THE GREAT CLUD MIGRATION

Your Roadmap to
Cloud Computing,
Big Data and Linked Data

MICHAEL C. DACONTA

Table of Contents

List of Figures

List of Tables

Introduction

"Computing may someday be organized as a public utility just as the telephone system is a public utility."[1]
                                - Professor John McCarthy, 1961

Cloud computing is here and growing rapidly. While still in its early stages, this trend will affect every IT professional and executive as every company shifts their IT resources from private computing resources to cloud-based resources. This will require many applications to be migrated to the cloud environment and it is that "Great Cloud Migration" that is the focus of this book. Before you are done reading, you will understand all the key aspects of Cloud computing, Big Data and Linked Data; why and how to migrate your applications to these new platforms and a smart roadmap for doing so! Let's examine how this book is organized to accomplish those goals.

Organization of this Book

This book is designed to inform and instruct both business managers and technical managers in understanding cloud, big data and linked data so that you can either devise a cloud strategy or assist in developing such a strategy. Furthermore, technical implementers will also get value out of this book as there is enough technical depth to demonstrate the feasibility of the concepts and how they provide value to the organization. Let's examine the purpose and objective of each chapter:

- <u>Chapter One: Yet Another Computing Revolution?</u> This chapter will demonstrate how cloud computing is

---

[1] McCarthy, John; MIT's Centennial Celebration Speech; 1961.

the beginning of another revolution in computing and the impacts of that revolution on businesses and individuals. We will explore the "Post-PC" architecture and the Cloud tipping point to get an idea of when these massive changes will be the dominant computing platform.

- <u>Chapter Two: Cloud 101</u>. This chapter will go over all the basics of cloud computing and give you a good understanding of the foundations of this new technology. We will closely examine all the details of the National Institute of Standards and Technology (NIST) definition of cloud computing to include the meaning of Infrastructure, Platform and Software as a Service. Delving even deeper, you will understand the elements of virtualization and how a hypervisor works. Finally, we will examine other cloud definitions and frameworks that offer alternative perspectives on what cloud computing is.

- <u>Chapter Three: Big Data 101</u>. This chapter will provide an in-depth understanding of what big data is, how its components work together and where it is going from here. You will learn how the data cloud is taking shape to improve business decisions. To round out your understanding we will also cover the history of big data and delve into the mechanics of components like key-value stores and columnar databases. We will close the chapter with a case study that demonstrates how big data can be leveraged to gain a competitive advantage.

- <u>Chapter Four: Linked Data 101</u>. This chapter will examine linked data and linked open data and how this technology relates to big data and cloud computing. It will also examine the trends pushing this technology, specifically, the popularity of social networking and open government data (aka government transparency). As in other 101 chapters, we will examine the history of linked data, the definition of linked data, its implementation and end with an illustrative case study.

- Chapter Five: Application Migration To The Cloud. This chapter will examine the process, method and ramifications of migrating your legacy applications to various cloud environments. We will cover IaaS, PaaS and SaaS migrations and examine case studies of actual migrations. Additionally, we will reveal some of the challenges with migrating applications and other complex issues to include data migration and cloud security. Finally, the chapter will conclude by examining the emerging area of cloud brokers and how they ease application migration, solution provisioning and cloud interoperability.

- Chapter Six: Your Cloud Computing Roadmap. This chapter will provide you with a specific, detailed approach to implementing the cloud in your organization. The strategy is broken down into three major phases of Assessment, Architecture and Action (a "triple-A" strategy). This strategy is measured and conservative in order to ensure your company has a smooth transition to the cloud based on a solid foundation. As part of the architecture section, we examine the major components of architecture, including Cloud architectural patterns that will provide your organization with a solid foundation to move to the cloud. Finally, we end the chapter by polishing our crystal ball to envision the future of the cloud.

- **Conclusion**. The final chapter will recap all the key topics and highlight the key takeaways from the book. This short chapter will serve as both a refresher and stress the lessons learned.

Acknowledgements

The writing of a book is never an individual accomplishment. There are always so many people that contribute in ways big and small. Here I'd like to take a moment to thank the people who have helped me during the writing of this book:

- My dear wife Lynne who is the best partner and team-mate a man could ever hope for. She gives me the strength each day to work hard for our family. Our love burns brighter now than ever before and I happily look forward to our future together.

- My children, CJ, Gregory and Samantha who have grown into fine young adults. I'm proud of whom you have become and confident you will succeed in life.

- My family who are always there for me, especially, my brothers Joseph and Christian Daconta. I enjoy our weekly talks.

- My copyeditors Heather Poirier and Claire Hoffman. Thank you for helping me produce a high quality book!

- My colleagues at InCadence Strategic Solutions who I have the pleasure of working with every day: Sandy Corbett, Anthony Iasso, Al Danis, Larry Campbell, Peter Ward, John McIntyre, Don Acker, Jesse Fullerton, Derek Clemenzi, Ian Nathan, Ericka Shirley,

Vanessa Davidson, Kimberly Rogers, Ashley Sullivan, Caitlyn Kish, Derek Croxton, Tom Hawes and many others. Special thanks to Sandy Corbett and Anthony Iasso who are both colleagues and friends. It is an honor and privilege to work with passionate people who love technology. Speaking of passion and enthusiasm, kudos and thanks to our motivated young interns: Nick Iasso, Philip Mulford and Jamie Dyer. Keep on Coding!

♦ My colleagues at Government Computer News who are a pleasure to work with in writing my monthly "Reality Check" columns to include Paul McCloskey, Kevin McCaney and David Hubler (a fellow NYU alumnus).

♦ My other professional colleagues with whom I have worked this past year to include Rob Hickey, Susan Parker, Sharon Claridge, Carrie Wibben, Christy Wilder, Dr. John Capps, John Sanders, Justin Albrechtsen, Allison Barretta and Samantha Smith-Pritchard. Special thanks to my colleagues in the Florida Department of Law Enforcement to include Penny Kincannon, Mark Zadra, Ian Anderson and J.D. Ross. Special thanks to my Arizona colleagues Kathy Debolt and Gary Jones.

♦ My friends and fellow Jiu Jitsu athletes who keep things fun! Thanks to my friends Danny Proko, Charlie Sowell, Adam Silver, Kevin Smith, and Jude Luellen for your camaraderie and goofing around! Thanks to my friends at Premier Fight Center for pushing me to be a better athlete to include Master Leo Dalla, Chris Lattanzi, Vu Tran, Amando Carigo, Todd

Hubbel, Scott Salb, Kenny Goebel, Tom Lucas, Matt Helle and many others at the gym!

Again, even though the list above is long, I am sure to be forgetting many people to whom I apologize.

Feedback

This book is the start of an important dialogue:

- Website - a set of pages on my personal website http://www.daconta.us/Articles/gcm.html will cover general information about the book, errata, and projects related to the book.

- Blog – I will be regularly blogging about application migration to the cloud on this new blog: http://greatcloudmigration.wordpress.com/. I look forward to your comments and feedbacks on the various posts throughout the year.

- Email – you are welcome to contact me via email at michael.daconta@gmail.com. I look forward to your reporting of errors, feedback, constructive comments and suggestions for improvements. Please prefix the subject of your email with "[GCM Feedback]" so I don't confuse it with spam.

I encourage you to take advantage of these collaboration methods and join me in designing a more effective digital future.

Best Wishes,

Michael C. Daconta
Woodbridge, Virginia

Chapter One: Yet Another Computing Revolution?

"'Cloud-computing' is a dynamic computing paradigm where the boundaries of computing are determined by rationale provided by technological, economic, organizational and security requirements."[2]
- Ramnath K. Chellapa, 1997,
first use of the term "Cloud computing"

Cloud computing will change everything – again. The history of computers is rife with "revolutions" – the Electronic Numerical Integrator And Computer (ENIAC) heralded the first computer revolution with a new era of "thinking machines"; the personal computer revolution enabled the average person to own a computer; the internet revolution ushered in global communication and the World Wide Web (WWW); and now, just when we think computing has "settled down", we have a brand new revolution to upturn the apple cart. Is it hyperbole to use the term "revolution" to express the changes augured by the emergence of cloud computing? No, on the contrary, the magnitude of societal, economic and cultural changes caused directly or indirectly by cloud computing will most likely be larger than those previous computing revolutions due to the sheer number of devices and, in turn, people affected by those changes. The three major areas of impact are cost, connectivity and big data. Computing-as-a-utility changes what is possible with computing in terms of processing power and also changes the cost basis for metering and the delivery of required resources only when they are needed. Thus, the general cost of computing will drastically decrease while the ubiquity of computing

---

[2] Intermediaries in Cloud-Computing: A New Computing Paradigm; Ramnath K. Chellappa. Presented at the INFORMS meeting in Dallas in 1997.

drastically increases. This can be seen today with web 2.0 startups taking advantage of the "information utility" to expand computing capability only when their user base grows to require it. Thus, they get to avoid a large cash outlay up front and they use computing resources just like they use electricity – they only pay for what they use and only use it when they need it. The cloud offers this metered billing on a per-hour basis; for example, in 2011 I was paying 26 cents an hour for a Windows 2008 Server to run a web application. So, metered billing, like the electric meter depicted in Figure 1, will continue to get finer grained (possibly billing per minute or per second) and cheaper (Amazon lowered its cloud prices nineteen times in six years[3]).

Figure 1 An Electric Meter[4]

Secondly, the revolution will enable an increase in the number of mobile devices, sensors, in-auto devices and home automation devices as the glue to tie them all together. We see this in the

[3] Whittaker, Zack; ZDNet; "Amazon drops cloud prices worldwide (again)"; March 6, 2012; http://www.zdnet.com/blog/btl/amazon-drops-cloud-prices-worldwide-again/70881
[4] Photo in Creative Commons by Laura Gilmore (with permission). http://www.flickr.com/photos/genbug/

mobile space where personal content such as books, videos and music are stored in the cloud so that they are accessible across smart phones, tablets and personal computers. Finally, the cloud revolution will impact every business, government agency and non-profit organization with the ability to analyze and visualize huge volumes of data in "real time"[5]. This advent of "big data" applications was impossible before the cloud and is having a significant impact on numerous industries from healthcare to retail to finance and many others. So, while the computer industry has had a string of revolutions throughout its history, the cloud revolution completes the transition from expensive and exclusive resources (mainframes) to ubiquitous, on-demand, metered services (the Computing or Information Utility). Part of this transition is a move away from personal computers to what some, most notably Apple, have called the "Post-PC" Architecture.

The Post-PC Architecture

"I think there's going to be tremendous revolution, you know, in the experiences of the post-PC devices."[6] – Steve Jobs, 2007

The terms "Post-PC", "Post-PC Devices" and "Post-PC Era"[7] have come into the mainstream through Steve Jobs, the former CEO of Apple, when describing where the company's new devices (iPod, iPhone and especially the iPad[8]) fit in the current computing ecosystem. While some, especially Microsoft and PC manufacturers, have been critical of this; most people agree and the trends point to a decline in personal computer sales as other, cheaper and more convenient, devices proliferate. More

---

[5] By this I mean "real time" in a business sense of hours and minutes and not in a "hardware sense" of milliseconds and nanoseconds.
[6] Steve Jobs Interview, All Things Digitial Conference,
http://allthingsd.com/20070530/d5-gates-jobs-interview/
[7] http://en.wikipedia.org/wiki/Post-PC_era
[8] iPhone, iPod and iPad are © of Apple, Inc.

important than whether the PC will decline or not is how a Post-PC era is changing the way we compute, how we get our information and how we run our businesses. The central components of the Post-PC Architecture are mobile devices, the cloud (or clouds), sensors and social networks. Of these components, mobile devices (as depicted in Figure 2) are the most immediate and primary driver that is drastically reshaping both the client and server side of the architectural equation.

Figure 2 iPhone Driving the Post-PC Architecture[9]

Of these changes, the most important is the drive towards "natural interfaces" like gesture and voice. But not to be dismissed is the plethora of sensors (some of them inside those mobile devices) that can monitor, measure and signal in every corner of the globe. Thus, from a sheer numbers perspective, the Post-PC Architecture is the realization of ubiquitous computing.

---

[9] Photo in Creative Commons by Yutaka Tsutano (with permission).
http://www.flickr.com/people/ivyfield/

To accommodate that volume and enable easy sharing between any type of client device requires an equally ubiquitous server solution that is ever-present, contextually aware and fast (regardless of load) – enter the cloud. Above and beyond this proliferation of hardware is a new higher bar for software platforms that are smart, social-by-design, exhibit situational awareness, and leverage vast amounts of data.

To satisfy the requirements levied by these Post-PC components, the key characteristics of a Post-PC Architecture are scalability, semantics and security. The characteristic of scalability is required for the cloud to serve the massive numbers of devices and sensors in near-real time. The cloud will allow device convergence and interoperability across every organization in ways never thought imaginable. The characteristic of semantics will be the glue between each component in order to enable the devices to understand the whole, understand their part to play and to then act appropriately in the current situation. That is what we mean by "situational awareness" and to do this requires an understanding of "localized context". For example, if I say to Siri, "Call my wife", it understands that I am married, which contact in my address book represents my spouse, and which phone number I most often call her on. I recommend everyone read the Siri patent[10] to see how the semantic web techniques I wrote about in my 2004 book entitled, The Semantic Web, have finally crossed the chasm and are another key driver of the Post-PC architecture. So, with the scalability of the cloud enabling greater semantics, both of them combined will enable major breakthroughs in security. Sensor, device and Cloud components form a new type of multi-machine operating system that is being designed as we speak. But this multi-machine OS will be free to look beyond processor, memory and storage limitations towards robust and built-in solutions for identity (including biometrics), provenance,

---

[10] http://www.patentlyapple.com/patently-apple/2012/01/apple-introduces-us-to-siri-the-killer-patent.html

continuous monitoring, and cradle-to-grave mandatory security context. So, while there are many changes ahead in this Post-PC Era, the opportunity to forge a secure, scalable and semantic architecture is well worth the price.

The Cloud Tipping Point

Cloud computing is shifting to a new level of acceptance, adoption and competition. In this section, I will examine four waves of cloud adoption and speculate on when/if it will hit a tipping point.

These four waves of adoption are overlapping and not sequential in time:

• **Wave 1, The "Startup" Wave** – this wave of adopters is composed of startup companies developing interactive "Web 2.0" sites that can scale in both capacity and cost as their user base (and hopefully revenue) scales. The primary driver for this group is metered billing as it best fits their business model. Evidence of this is seen when any major cloud provider goes down and knocks out a huge swathe of our favorite internet sites.

• **Wave 2, The "Commodity" Wave** – this wave of adopters is business and government organizations primarily interested in reducing data center costs via IaaS clouds. The primary drivers of this wave are data center self-service and data center consolidation. This will witness a growth and consolidation of IaaS providers (evidenced by Go Daddy recently dropping out of this space) and eventually culminate in either de-facto or formal IaaS standards.

• **Wave 3, The "Consumer" Wave** – this wave of adopters is average individuals that subscribe to cloud services directly without knowing or caring how it works. A recent Citrix Cloud Survey found that 51% of respondents believe that stormy weather would interfere with their cloud computing. When this wave occurs in earnest, that percentage will be lowered dramatically. The drivers of this wave are multiple devices (tablets, smart phones, cars, sensors, etc.) and the desired simplicity of them all seamlessly working together. This is the culmination of Software-as-a-Service (SaaS) with iCloud and Xbox Live paving the way.

• **Wave 4, The "Enterprise" Wave** – this wave of adopters is when all businesses (small, mid-sized and large) target the majority of their IT development, including mission critical applications, to a cloud platform. The key drivers for this wave are cloud interoperability and reliability. If the cloud is to fulfill its promise of a "computing utility" similar to the electric grid then businesses, consumers and governments will have no fear of switching providers.

It should be clear that each of these waves of adopters both encourages and supports the next wave. If you plotted these waves as normal distributions with the Y-axis being adoption and the X-axis being time, you could draw a line at Time T where all four waves intersect somewhere in their lifecycle as depicted in Figure 3.

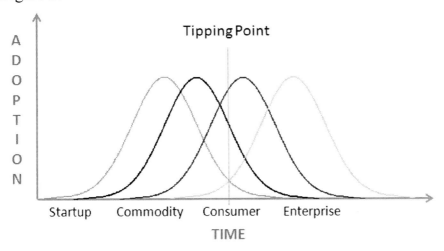

Figure 3 The Cloud Adoption Tipping Point

At that point – where all of these waves of adoption are either continuing or have begun – will be the tipping point where the cloud becomes the dominant computing platform. Today we are at the zenith of Wave 1, about 15-25% into Wave 2 and at the starting point of Wave 3. Of course, there is the possibility that either a catalyst or disruptive event could hasten or hinder any or all of these waves and thereby hasten or hinder the tipping point. While the U.S. and European governments are trying to play the role of catalyst, the evidence shows that the first two waves have been and are progressing with almost no influence or acceleration from their participation. The marketplace of providers and mindshare of developers is the only thing currently influencing these trends.

The Great Cloud Migration

Now that we understand the major forces driving this new computing-as-a-utility revolution, we come to the key point of this book – assisting organizations in devising a roadmap to this revolution and more specifically assisting in the migration of their existing legacy applications to this new cloud environment. If you agree that Cloud computing is a new stage in the evolution of computing, it will affect every application running in your organization. In essence, every application may need to be migrated to this new environment. How to migrate your applications to the Cloud is the focus of Chapter Five. Crafting a roadmap to migrate all of these applications in an orderly fashion is the focus of Chapter Six.

Now that we understand how and when cloud computing will impact every organization and individual in the foreseeable future, it is time to delve into the "what" and understand the details of the form and function of this new computing revolution!

.

Chapter Two: Cloud 101

"For those of you not familiar with cloud computing, here is a brief explanation. There was a time when every household, town, or village had its own water well. Today, shared public utilities give us access to clean water by simply turning on the tap. Cloud computing works a lot like our shared public utilities. However, instead of water coming from a tap, users access computing power from a pool of shared resources."[11]

- Vivek Kundra, Federal CIO, 2010

What is the Cloud?

The term cloud originated as an analogy for the internet because network diagrams depicted the internet via a cloud symbol as depicted in Figure 4.

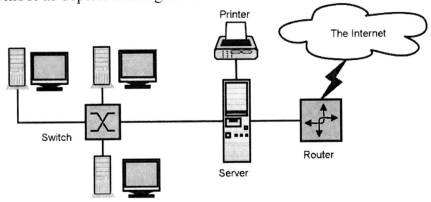

Figure 4 The Internet Depicted as a Cloud[12]

Such symbolism depicting the internet as a cloud signifies that the computing resources were external to your organization or "out there". This notion of not knowing where something is

---

[11] http://www.whitehouse.gov/blog/2010/05/13/moving-cloud
[12] Image in the Creative Commons by SilverStar (with permission). http://en.wikipedia.org/wiki/File:Sample-network-diagram.png

being executed embodies the notion of a shared utility – for example, where is the website Amazon.com running? On what physical server and in what data center is it running? The answer is that people don't know and don't care. In fact, they shouldn't care as long as they get the service (in this case, a virtual storefront) they need. Thus, running things on the internet is equivalent to the question of "where does your electricity or water come from?" Again, the answer is "don't know and don't care". Besides this "location independence" of compute resources (like processing, storage and network bandwidth), the notion of elasticity is central to the cloud and central to the notion of the cloud as a "Computing Resources Utility". In relation to your electricity, no one tells you how much or how little to use. That is up to you and that same flexibility is central to the cloud. In the cloud, computing resources are elastic, like a rubber band, in that they can scale up or scale down when needed. So, while we will examine the National Institute of Standards and Technology's (NIST) formal definition of cloud computing later in this chapter, for now it is more important to have an informal understanding of the cloud as a service provider, like an electric utility, that can provide various types of computing resources as an on-demand, elastic, measured and metered service. In short, the cloud is "Computing as a Utility". Table 1 provides a list of computing resources and an example of a provider that offers them as a service.

Table 1 Computing Resources available as an Online Service

Compute Resource	Service Provider
Office Applications	Google Docs, Microsoft Office 365
Email	Gmail, Microsoft Office 365
File Storage	Egnyte, Rackspace, Google's Gdrive
Virtual Servers	Amazon EC2, Google Compute, GoGrid

Compute Resource	Service Provider
Data Storage, Database Services	Amazon Simple DB, database.com
Software Development	Salesforce.com, Google AppEngine, Microsoft Azure

Let's examine some of the examples from Table 1 in more detail. Complete software applications (like office applications and email) running via a web browser and provided on a per-user, subscription-style basis are replacing the traditional shrink-wrapped installed software for many types of software. Early success stories in this space are Gmail, Google's email client, and Google Docs which is Google's office productivity suite (word processing, spreadsheets, presentations, etc.). The key differentiators for software applications in the cloud are subscription purchasing, no installation, no maintenance, and user's data is stored in the cloud (which makes collaboration easier while also raising some security concerns). Whereas these software applications in the cloud are at one end of the computing resources spectrum (akin to a "finished product"), at the other end, the "raw" resources used to create those applications are also provisioned as a service, metered and sold. Figure 5 depicts this "Computing Resources Spectrum".

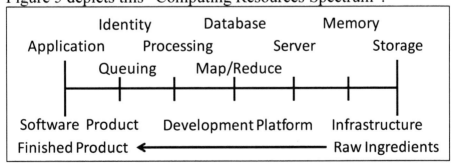

Figure 5 Computing Resources Spectrum

Those low-level or "raw" computing resources are called computing "infrastructure" similar to the plumbing or electrical wiring in a house. The largest vendor of these "Infrastructure" services is Amazon.com via its Amazon Web Services (http://aws.amazon.com/). As you can see in Figure 5, computing resources progress from those infrastructure services towards building a finished end-product of a cloud-enabled software product or application. We will cover the middle area in ensuing sections that cover the cloud as a development platform and the chapter on Big Data will cover the parallel processing algorithm called "MapReduce". While the reality of services offered is a little mix and match and messier than the diagram shows, the basic idea of a set of building block services offered as online commodities is sound. Let's highlight two very popular types of infrastructure services: file storage and virtual servers. File storage as an online service is when a company sells disk space, usually on a per-gigabyte basis, for a monthly fee. My company, InCadence Strategic Solutions, Inc., uses this type of service to provide collaborative file storage for all our company documents as depicted in Figure 6.

Figure 6 Egnyte Cloud-based File Storage

Salesforce.com is a leader in providing a Cloud development platform to businesses which they call the "Salesforce Platform". Their marketing on their website states that you can develop your apps on their platform five times faster and at half the cost of traditional software development. They have a robust development environment including a downloadable Programming Editor, their own programming language (called Apex), and a large set of pre-built libraries to leverage. In essence, they are attempting three things with cloud-based software development: first, remove the complex part of programming like multi-threading and security; second, build scalable, on-demand applications out of the box; and third, develop applications faster than before. The only downside at this time is that all of these cloud-based development environments (Salesforce, Google, Microsoft) are all proprietary and therefore lock you in to that vendor's cloud with no ability to migrate your application to other vendors' cloud. We will discuss this further in Chapter 5.

Finally, let's discuss subscription-based software applications in the cloud. One of the best examples of this is Microsoft Office 365, the online version of the world's most popular office suite. Just as Microsoft had shifted the company in the early nineties to integrate its products with the internet (and develop Internet Explorer), Microsoft has pivoted to integrate its offerings with the Cloud environment. The office suite has received good reviews in terms of its functionality with the typical two caveats that your data is stored on Microsoft servers (some see this as a good thing while others do not) and the requirement to be connected to the internet (or online) to get any work done. The requirement to be connected is a persistent problem for this category of software but is being addressed in HTML 5 with a database in the browser and improved offline functionality. Now that we have an understanding of how the Cloud acts like a public utility, let's examine the history of cloud computing to see how we arrived at this point.

The History of Cloud Computing

The history of cloud computing is intertwined with the history of computing in general, and as we examine the key events in that history you will see the trends that emerged and naturally evolved into what we have today. The beginnings of computer history began with the ENIAC in 1946 and more generally with the era of large mainframe computers. As quoted in the introduction, Professor John McCarthy discussed the possibility of computing as a utility in 1961 as depicted below in Figure 7. More important though than the general concept and one of the foundational underpinnings of cloud computing is the virtualization of an operating system (OS) in order to run multiple copies of the OS simultaneously inside a single system to facilitate time sharing of the mainframe. Virtualization was invented for the IBM System 360 mainframe as part of the CP-40 operating system (followed quickly by the CP-67 OS) in 1964.

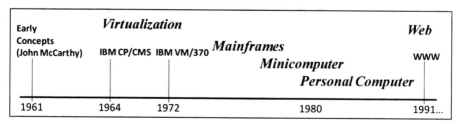

Figure 7 Origins of Cloud Computing

Virtualization is the creation of a virtual, not actual, version of a physical thing (like a computing platform, or disk storage). In the case of virtualizing an operating system, the computer creates copies of virtual hardware and in essence fools the OS (which is software) to run on the virtual hardware instead of the real hardware so that it can run multiple copies of the OS simultaneously. This "control software" that runs the multiple operating systems is called a "hypervisor". It is interesting to note that both time sharing of a computer amongst multiple users for a centralized computing resource (in this case the mainframe) and virtualization were technologies invented in the 1960's. What is old is new again. Of course with cloud computing, these techniques have been perfected to add numerous other characteristics, chief among them is scalability across hundreds and even thousands of small, cheap (commodity) machines. In fact, the rest of the early computing history as depicted in Figure 7 involves that trend towards miniaturization and personalization of the hardware so that every business and eventually every individual could own their own computing resources. Of course, this shows a key difference between time sharing and cloud computing because time sharing involved only getting a small slice of computing time because you had to share it with other users and even potentially get bumped off by a higher priority user. Well, users wanted their own resources and thus the drive towards cheaper and smaller computers – first minicomputers and then personal computers. Figure 7 ends with the introduction in 1991 of the World Wide Web which began the reversal of distributed computing by tying everyone together in a single "sharing" platform or web. As you can see, this tension between centralized computing and distributed computing has swung back and forth as the forces of control versus collaboration waxed and waned. In essence, cloud computing combines the best of both. The web was a watershed event for cloud computing because it spearheaded the movement online and away from computing on the desktop. Now let's examine the recent history of cloud computing as depicted in Figure 8.

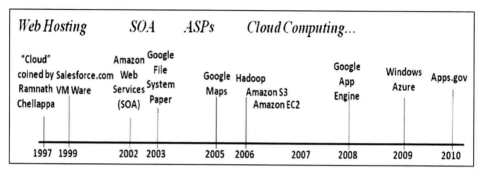

Figure 8 Recent History of Cloud Computing

As shown in Figure 8, the term cloud was first coined by Ramnath Chellappa in a 1997 academic lecture. More importantly, shortly thereafter two companies entered the market, Salesforce.com to sell online Customer Relationship Management (CRM) software and VMWare to sell virtualization software. At that time, these two companies did not really know they were in the "cloud" business. Additionally, Amazon.com opened its data center software to the world via a set of standard web services called Amazon Web Services. Again, this was more of a Service Oriented Architecture play initially started to increase customized storefront by offering up the Amazon "back-end" software to new front-end websites. A key watershed event occurred in October 2003, when Google published an academic paper on its "Google File System"[13]. The paper demonstrated how the Google engineers created a distributed file system that could span across hundreds or thousands of inexpensive computers to store massive data sets. One year later, in 2004 (though not shown on the diagram), Google released another academic paper on a parallel programming algorithm called "MapReduce"[14]. The importance of these papers cannot be overstated. It demonstrated a significant shift away from operating system functionality that controls a single machine to

---

[13] Sanjay Ghemawat, Howard Gobioff, and Shun-Tak Leung, The Google File System, http://research.google.com/archive/gfs.html

[14] Jeffrey Dean and Sanjay Ghemawat, MapReduce: Simplified Data Processing on Large Clusters, http://research.google.com/archive/mapreduce.html

operating system functionality (like a file system) that spans multiple machines (truly scalable for global scale capabilities). An open source version of these Google technologies, called Hadoop and programmed in the cross-platform Java programming language, was released two years later in 2006. Hadoop is the dominant platform for creating "Big Data" applications. Before that, Google caused another watershed event, this time in the area of software applications in its release of Google Maps. Google Maps was the most feature rich and advanced web application that used an asynchronous method to fetch XML data behind the scenes (later called the "AJAX" method) so that the web interface was smooth and not hampered by page refreshes. Google Maps demonstrated that web applications could be as feature-rich as desktop applications. Google Maps truly marked the beginning of the end for what was called "fat apps" on the desktop. This meant that online web applications were the way to go and spawned a large programming movement around web applications that used this technology called Asynchronous Javascript and XML or AJAX. At this point, we are starting to see the tectonic shifts in the computing landscape shifting away from individual desktops to web-based functionality and in the next phase we will see the shift away from physical servers to virtual ones. In 2006, Amazon.com continued its evolution beyond an electronic storefront into an IT powerhouse with the introduction of Amazon Simple Storage Service (S3) for cloud-based data storage and Amazon Elastic Compute Cloud (EC2) for the creation and management of virtual servers. The Amazon EC2 has become extremely popular for its ease of use and low cost. The AWS EC2 Management Console for launching and monitoring a set of virtual instances (each instance being one instantiation of a virtual server) is depicted in Figure 9 (only part of the console window is shown).

Figure 9 AWS EC2 Management Console

In Figure 9, the table is the list of running server instances, each with its own Internet Protocol (IP) address so that it can be accessed over the internet just as if it resided in your own data center. Below the table of instances are the monitoring graphs for the one selected instance showing CPU utilization, disk reads and writes and network bandwidth consumption. Providing these virtual servers and storage available online has become known as Infrastructure-as-a-Service (IaaS) as we will discuss in the next section. As we mentioned before, besides offering virtual servers, companies then began offering programming environments targeting software developers to build cloud-based applications on their platform. Specifically in 2008, Google launched the Google App Engine and Microsoft followed a year later with Microsoft Azure. These vendors launched a different type of cloud service that targets their installed base of developers with an option to develop scalable cloud apps. Since writing scalable apps is hard, these offerings simplify the process of software development and are therefore attractive to developers and IT managers. These types of services are called Platform-as-a-Service (PaaS) which we will define in the next section. Finally, in 2010 the United States Government launched a cloud computing portal called Apps.gov that showcased cloud based applications and services. The initial launch focused mostly on completed software applications (like email, productivity applications, Salesforce applications, etc.) available for use on a subscription basis. This type of complete applications available in the cloud is known as Software-as-a-Service (SaaS) which we will define in the next section. The trends revealed in this recent history of cloud computing is the shift to web applications combined with a shift to Service Oriented Architectures (SOA), which basically switched the focus from desktop apps to online applications. The World Wide Web and the network became the new development platform of choice. Now we are ready to more formally define cloud computing.

The Definition of Cloud Computing

While there are numerous definitions of cloud computing, we will begin this section by examining the most widely used definition which was developed in an iterative, community fashion by the US Government's National Institute of Standards and Technology (NIST).

"Cloud computing is a model for enabling ubiquitous, convenient, on-demand network access to a shared pool of configurable computing resources (e.g., networks, servers, storage, applications, and services) that can be rapidly provisioned and released with minimal management effort or service provider interaction. This cloud model is composed of five essential characteristics, three service models, and four deployment models."[15]

This cloud computing framework is sometimes called the 3-4-5 model as that follows the count of service models, deployment models and characteristics. The service models are Software as a Service (SaaS), Platform as a Service (PaaS), and Infrastructure as a Service (IaaS). The three service models are depicted below in Figure 10.

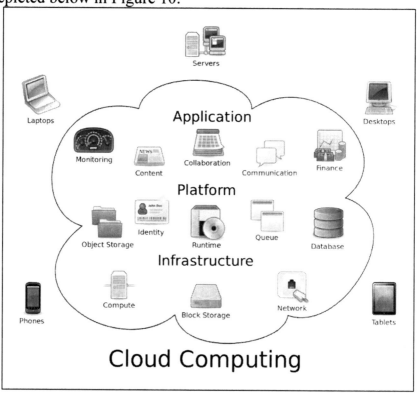

Figure 10 Three Types of Cloud Computing[16]

---

[15] Peter Mell and Timothy Grance, The NIST Definition of Cloud Computing, NIST Special Publication 800-145. http://www.nist.gov/itl/csd/cloud-102511.cfm
[16] Image in the creative commons by Sam Johnson.
http://en.wikipedia.org/w/index.php?title=File:Cloud_computing.svg;

Figure 10 clearly shows the three types of cloud computing that are part of the NIST definition with Application being equivalent to Software as a Service. This diagram is from the Wikipedia article on Cloud computing and serves as a useful overview of the NIST definition. Below those major categories, the diagram breaks down the service offerings into more specific, though only representative and not exhaustive, resource offerings. Many of these computing resources we discussed when covering the computing resources spectrum. Let's examine some of the new ones briefly here and then again in more detail in the sections below. Under the Application Cloud Services (aka Software as a Service), we see categories of applications like finance applications, communication applications, collaboration, etc. These categories are commonplace and self-explanatory. Under the Platform Cloud Services (aka Platform as a Service), we see several items that may be unfamiliar. Object Storage is a special type of data storage for object-oriented programs. Identity services are for user management, authentication and authorization. A runtime refers to the ability to execute parts of a program in a scalable manner. Queue services enable different executing programs to communicate using a queue to pass messages between them. Database services provided either Structured Query Language (SQL) or NoSQL type data storage. The Infrastructure Cloud Services (aka Infrastructure as a Service) also use slightly different terminology than we have used before; however, we can easily translate them. The Compute service is equivalent to virtual server computing resources or virtualization. Block storage is slightly different than file storage as it is a lower-level service. Block storage is equivalent to a network accessible hard drive and therefore can be used for any type of storage to include a file system (for file storage) or database storage. Network cloud services are things like load balancing, security (like secure sockets layer, SSL), and firewalls.

The characteristics of the NIST definition are on-demand self-service, broad network access, resource pooling, rapid elasticity and measured service. Most of these characteristics are self explanatory. The resource pooling characteristic refers to the idea that resources are shared with multiple consumers and are location-independent. All of these characteristics were covered in our discussion of Cloud computing as a utility as they represent the characteristics that we expect from a shared utility. The deployment models are private cloud, community cloud, public cloud or hybrid cloud. We will discuss the details of these deployment strategies in a section below.

Software as a Service

The NIST definition for SaaS is "The capability provided to the consumer is to use the provider's applications running on a cloud infrastructure. The applications are accessible from various client devices through either a thin client interface, such as a web browser (e.g., web-based email), or a program interface." The key use case for SaaS is that the customer gets a complete application with no installation and monthly, per-user billing. Amazon Web Services (AWS) currently operates a marketplace[17], and many vendors (like Oracle and HP) have SaaS pages on their respective websites. Additionally, Salesforce.com has an AppExchange [18] Marketplace and Microsoft has an Azure Marketplace[19]. In 2012, the General Services Administration ran a site called Apps.gov to display SaaS offerings broken down by category. Figure 11 is a simple rendering of what that "catalog" type site looks like. It has a similar look and feel to the AWS marketplace which also advertizes SaaS offerings.

---

[17] https://aws.amazon.com/marketplace
[18] https://appexchange.salesforce.com/
[19] http://datamarket.azure.com/

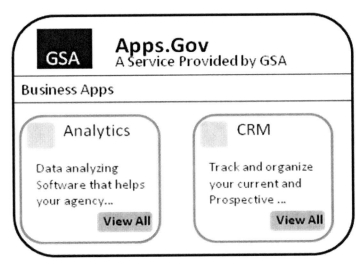

Figure 11 Apps.gov SaaS offerings

Figure 11 only shows two of many categories that were offered for SaaS on Apps.gov [20]. The pricing for SaaS applications can vary widely from a yearly subscription for a block of users, per-user per month, multi-year contracts, free service with support fees, and many, many other variations. Caveat emptor (buyer beware) must be your motto because while SaaS pricing is supposed to save money, especially up-front costs, it may come down to how well you negotiate.

Platform as a Service

The NIST definition of PaaS is "The capability provided to the consumer is to deploy onto the cloud infrastructure consumer-created or acquired applications created using programming languages, libraries, services, and tools supported by the provider." The key use case for PaaS is for your developers to be able to rapidly build scalable cloud applications. PaaS provides a cloud development platform that simplifies the

---

[20] As of the publication of this book, Apps.gov now redirects you to http://cloud.cio.gov/ which is an informational site that helps Government managers to learn about, use, acquire, manage and secure the cloud.

process of application programming in general and cloud application programming in particular. Many vendors offer development platforms to include Google's AppEngine, Microsoft Azure, Grid Gain, Salesforce.com's Force platform and many others. One of the most mature platforms is the Force.com platform whose application development process and corresponding support services are depicted in Figure 12 below.

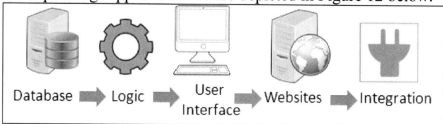

Figure 12 Force.com Application Development Process

Force.com enables developers to create scalable databases that run on their hardware via form-based wizards. This is very similar to the easy What-You-See-Is-What-You-Get (WYSIWYG) programming offered by visual database environments like Microsoft Access. The developer can then add validation, form logic, workflow and even advanced custom methods using either wizards or a Salesforce.com developed custom programming language called Apex. Apex has a Java-like syntax that should be familiar to many Java and Javascript developers. Unfortunately, Apex is also a proprietary and limited language (Salesforce documentation states that it is not a general purpose programming language). The purpose of the Apex language is to customize Salesforce applications and add business logic to either the database fields or to process user interface interactions. So, Figure 12 should actually show the Logic part in multiple places of the diagram; however, for simplicity's sake it only shows the logic in between the database and the user interface which is the traditional place for business logic in terms of the standard three-tier architecture (user interface to business logic to data storage). To develop the user interface, a Force.com developer builds a set of web pages using the Visual Force UI development [21] environment. With the Visual Force development environment it is easy to generate web pages with tables, images, maps and forms. Force.com ties all these elements together using a Model-View-Controller (MVC) pattern for connecting the visual elements (the view) to the data (the model) via some programming logic (the controller). Once the user interfaces are created, a programmer can register a public site on force.com and receive a Domain Name Service (DNS) name to create a public-facing website. Lastly, if the application needs to integrate with legacy applications, the Force.com platform has a large set of client-side Application Programming Interfaces in numerous popular languages to access the application's logic and data from external systems. Now let's switch to examining another vendor's Platform as a Service, Microsoft's Windows Azure.

The Windows Azure platform components are depicted below in Figure 13. The Windows Azure platform is a robust set of component services including multiple types of cloud computing. Let's examine each category of Windows Azure services and discuss each one. The Windows Azure Execution Models are different methods for executing a cloud application. Here is where Microsoft, in this diagram, goes beyond PaaS because the virtual machines offering would be considered an Infrastructure service (which we will discuss next) and the websites service is in line with traditional web hosting. Neither of those offerings fit the PaaS model. The third execution model, cloud services, divides a cloud applications operation into two types of roles: a web role or a worker role. A web role can display a web user interface (UI), where a worker role is for background (non-UI) processing. Both of these roles can be spun up in any quantity to facilitate scalability.

---

[21] http://www.salesforce.com/us/developer/docs/fundamentals/index.htm

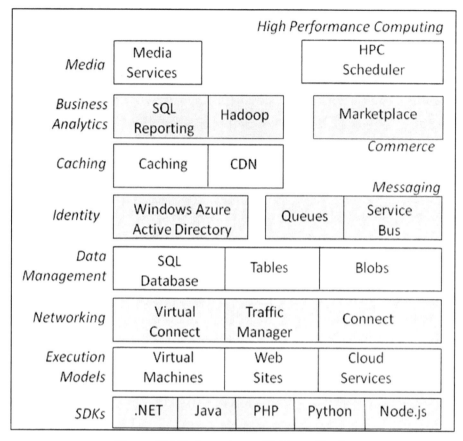

Figure 13 Windows Azure Platform Stack

The data management services offered range from the traditional Structured Query Language database, to simple key-value pair stores (also called NoSQL data stores), to simple Binary Large Objects (or BLOB) storage. For networking services, Microsoft offers two services to allow you to connect existing networks or individual computers to a Windows Azure network or application, and a Traffic Manager to perform smart load balancing. For Business Analytics services, Microsoft offers traditional SQL reporting (generating columnar based reports), or support for big data via running Hadoop Distributed File System (HDFS) nodes and the MapReduce parallel processing algorithm to produce huge volumes of data in real time. We will discuss

Hadoop and MapReduce in detail in the Big Data Chapter. For messaging services, Microsoft enables Windows Azure applications to communicate with each other via two methods: queues and a service bus. Queues are simply an instantiation of what their name implies, a list of messages processed in a particular order (usually first in, first out). A service bus is a special type of processing queue that offers a publish-and-subscribe mechanism on particular topics (this should not be confused with Java Enterprise Service Buses which are much more complex than this and outside the scope of this book). Caching services help applications reduce network requests for content that is requested over and over by keeping the most frequently requested content close and in memory. To facilitate this, Microsoft offers an in-memory caching service and a content delivery network that is aimed at serving up global content by saving copies in data centers around the world. Identity services enable applications to authenticate and authorize users to access functionality in their application. Microsoft offers this type of service via a cloud form of its very popular Active Directory Services called Windows Azure Active Directory. It is important to note that Active Directory is the leading platform for identity management amongst large corporations. The High Performance Computing service enables customers the ability to run large numbers of virtual machines simultaneously and implements a special message passing API to communicate between them. The Media services enable easy uploading, storing and encoding of streaming media (video, audio, etc.). The commerce services offer the Windows Azure marketplace as a global online market to sell SaaS applications. Again, Microsoft is blurring its offerings across SaaS, PaaS and IaaS. We will discuss this problem of vendors ignoring or blurring the categories of cloud computing (as well as over-using the "as-a-service" moniker) in a later section. Finally, the last category of Figure 13 shows that Microsoft supports multiple Software Development Kits (SDKs) for various languages and development platforms to include .NET (platform), Java (language and platform), PHP (language), Python (language), and Node.js (JavaScript server-side library).

Given the two detailed PaaS implementations we examined: Salesforce.com's Force.com platform and Microsoft's Windows Azure platform, you should have a good idea of the comprehensive software development environment that vendors are providing for developing cloud-based applications. The same type of robust environment is provided by numerous other vendors to include Google, Engine Yard, Bungee and many others. In general, all of these vendors are offering three key benefits – rapid application development, scalable cloud-based applications and easier application maintenance (installation and update). The target audience for PaaS is application developers (your IT shop). The downside of these many vendor offerings is that they are proprietary offerings with no ability to move an application development on one cloud platform to another vendor's platform. This could be considered PaaS' Achilles heel. Now, let's move on to the third and final type of cloud computing – Infrastructure as a Service.

Infrastructure as a Service

The NIST definition of IaaS is "The capability provided to the consumer is to provision processing, storage, networks, and other fundamental computing resources where the consumer is able to deploy and run arbitrary software, which can include operating systems and applications." While the NIST definition is accurate, it fails to highlight the central feature of IaaS which is the provisioning of virtual machines running your preferred operating system. Let's examine a simple use case to understand what this means. A development shop is beginning the development of a new corporate web application that will run on a Java-based application server and an open source database server. Typically, to develop such an application you would need to set up these two servers for the development environment, another set of two servers for the test environment and then two servers for the production environment. So, for this simple web application you would need to purchase six physical servers running either Windows Server software or some form of Linux (using Java, either would work fine). An alternative to purchasing six physical computers is to run your development and testing environments on virtual machines in either your private or a public cloud provider's data center. These virtual machines emulate a complete physical server so that the operating system runs in the same way it would run on the physical server, so when the developers remotely log in to the virtual machines there is absolutely no difference between the two. Figure 14 depicts how multiple virtual machines can execute on a single physical machine.

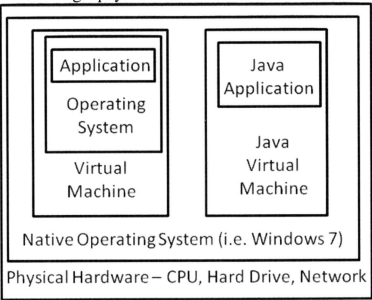

Figure 14 Virtual Machines on a Single Physical Machine

Figure 14 reveals two different types of virtual machines, a hardware virtual machine that can execute an entire operating system within it and a Java virtual machine (JVM) which only executes Java applications but enables Java applications to run on multiple platforms from different operating systems, to different types of hardware devices from smartphones to mainframes. Both types of virtual machines serve the purpose of creating a software container that emulates computer hardware to execute software in the same manner as if the software was executing "natively" (or on the physical hardware). As we covered in the Cloud Computing history section, these virtualization techniques have been around since the 1960's, steadily improving and becoming more commoditized. There are multiple high quality free and paid applications that enable you to run virtual machines on your personal computer (called "Desktop Virtualization") to include Microsoft's Virtual PC, Oracle's Virtual Box and VMWare Player. Figure 15 is a screenshot of executing Oracle's Virtual Box running Ubuntu (a version of the Linux operating system) on top of Windows 7.

Figure 15 Oracle's Virtual Box Running Ubuntu on Windows 7

As a simple exercise, I recommend you download the Virtual Box software (it is free[22]), then download an Operating System "Image" file and load the image into the Virtual Box to run it. The notion of an Operating System "Image" is important to virtualization because you may create multiple images of a system as you configure it with specific software. All of the commercial IaaS providers let you upload your own images once they have been configured the way you want them. So, for example, let's say you have a custom application you want to run in the cloud; instead of re-installing it each time, you can install the operating system, load and configure your application one time and then take a snapshot of the image and save it to load at a later time on one or more virtual servers. Although running some virtual machines or JVMs on your personal computer is a good introduction to virtualization, there are more architectural components necessary to bring virtualization to your data center and achieve greater utilization of your IT resources.

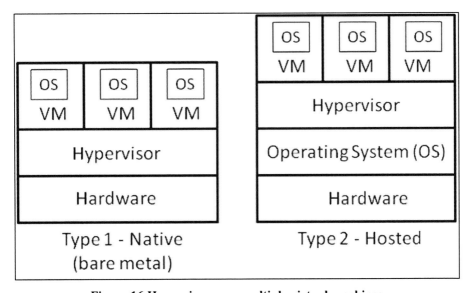

Figure 16 Hypervisor runs multiple virtual machines

[22] https://www.virtualbox.org/

Figure 16 introduces a new component to the virtualization architecture called a "Hypervisor" or a "Virtual Machine Manager" (VMM). Simply put, a hypervisor manages multiple virtual machines in the same manner that an operating system can spawn, manage and terminate multiple applications. The term hypervisor originated from IBM for the earliest virtual machine architecture on the System/370 mainframe. Additionally, you can see that there are two types of hypervisor, one type that runs directly on the hardware and one that runs on top of an operating system. In general, hypervisors running directly on the hardware will be more efficient. There are multiple commercial and open source hypervisors available, like VMWare vSphere, Xen and KVM (Kernel-Based Virtual Machine). Additionally, Microsoft is now shipping a built-in hypervisor with Windows Server 2012 called Microsoft Hyper-V Server. One other term that you will see is the notion of a "guest operating system"; these are the operating systems running inside the virtual machines that are being "hosted" by the Hypervisor.

Besides virtual machines, IaaS vendors also offer other low-level infrastructure services to include disk storage and networking services (like load balancers or firewalls). As we stated earlier, disk storage is often divided into block storage and file storage. Cloud based file storage is even being sold directly to consumers with offerings from Carbonite, Apple (iCloud), Amazon (Cloud Drive), DropBox and Google Drive. Pricing for all the IaaS services are very competitive as there are numerous large players in the IaaS market.

The key use case for IaaS is the ability to improve data center efficiency and agility by increasing the utilization of the hardware (no longer will a single application have data center physical hardware sitting idle during its non-peak hours) and enabling rapid experimentation in business units by allowing them to self-provision computing services for short-run tests or operations.

In addition to the Cloud Service models, the NIST definition specifies four deployment models: public, private, community and hybrid.

Cloud Deployment Models

Now that you are familiar with the cloud service models or "what" the cloud is (in terms of what it offers and to whom), let's examine the concept of "where" the cloud operates which entails examining where these services are located. The NIST definition specifies four types of deployment as depicted in Figure 17: private, community, public and hybrid.

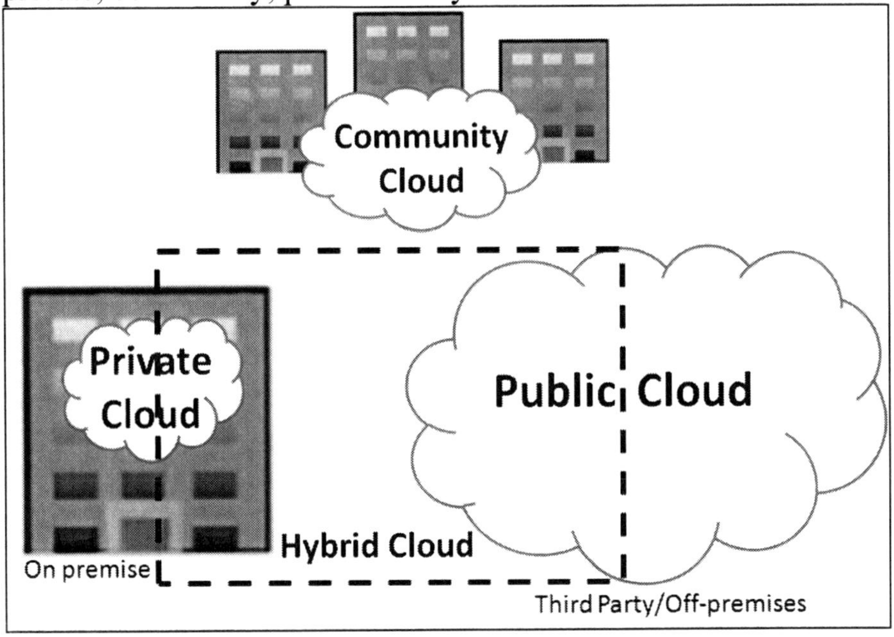

Figure 17 Cloud Deployment Models

Figure 17 shows the various deployment models as being primarily centered around the notion of location and control. The private cloud is provisioned for the exclusive use of a single organization and usually means that it is located on your premises in your data center (however, the NIST definition offers that it may be managed by someone else offsite as long as it is just for the use of a single organization). Today, private clouds are becoming extremely popular and there are numerous competing vendors offering private cloud implementations. Again, given the desire for control and increased security, most private cloud implementations are located on premises and under the control of the organization to which it belongs. That insures information security remains in control of the organization while still enabling the efficiencies of IaaS. A community cloud is very similar to a private cloud but is managed and operated by a group of organizations with a shared mission; for example, auto makers and the companies in their supply chain, or in the government the sixteen agencies that form the intelligence community. In a community cloud, one or more of the organizations may host the cloud for the community (again, NIST's definition suggests it could be hosted off premises and still fall under the definition). The public cloud is provisioned for use by the "general public" and services are consumed over the public internet. This is the first and most common form of the cloud given its history. The services are hosted externally from your organization by a cloud provider. And finally, the hybrid cloud is any combination of the above. The NIST definition adds that the cloud combinations should enable data and application portability between the clouds, but the standards to enable such portability are still immature. We will discuss cloud interoperability in Chapter Five. At this point, you should have a good understanding of how NIST defines cloud computing. The NIST definition is the most common definition of the cloud but not the only one. Let's examine some alternative definitions and perspectives on the cloud.

Other Cloud Definitions and Models

Besides the NIST definition, there are many other definitions of cloud computing. The Wikipedia definition is refreshingly simple: "Cloud computing is the use of computing resources (hardware and software) that are delivered as a service over a network (typically the Internet)." [23]   Of course, this simplified definition does not provide an understanding of the types of computing resources (like we did with the computing resources spectrum), nor does it discuss the deployment models besides the public internet. Besides multiple definitions, a more serious problem with Cloud computing is that it has become a marketing term where MBAs have twisted it to mean whatever they want it to mean. Furthermore, the "as-a-service" moniker has been expanded to numerous other areas like security as a service, data as a service, desktop as a service and many, many others.

In an attempt to stem this confusing mess of terminology, jargon and marketing hype, here is a more holistic definition of cloud computing:

> Cloud Computing is the **centralization** of computing services, delivered over a network, that offers greater hardware **efficiency**, improved data **sharing** across applications and application **scalability**. Cloud computing is implemented via multiple techniques to include virtualization, parallel processing across many commodity computers and new forms of data storage. A good analogy for this shift is when businesses moved from on-site power generation to electric utilities for reliable, inexpensive power.

---

[23] http://en.wikipedia.org/wiki/Cloud_computing

The above definition[24] covers both the how and the why of cloud computing by merging outcomes and implementation into the definition. It also incorporates the notion of data sharing and storage into the definition, which is a significant omission from the NIST definition. One final example of a cloud model that differs from the NIST definition is dividing a cloud implementation into three areas: a utility cloud, a desktop cloud[25] and a data cloud[26]. The utility cloud is synonymous with IaaS in that it allows a self-service approach to provisioning virtual machines in either a public or private cloud. The desktop cloud combines three features: a virtual desktop, an application marketplace for cloud applications and file storage in the cloud. The data cloud is the most divergent concept from the NIST definition and it seems to incorporate many data management concepts like metadata tagging of centralized data and distributed data systems like Hadoop to analyze and visualize huge volumes of data. The data cloud is emerging as a major type of cloud computing as it is synergistic with the "big data" movement. That brings us right to our next Chapter: Big Data 101 which will answer the key question: "What is Big Data?"

---

[24] It is important to note that the electric power generation analogy was put forth, in great detail, in Nicholas Carr's book, The Big Switch: Rewiring the world from Edison to Google.

[25] Cacas, Max; Signal Online; http://www.afcea.org/content/?q=node/10195

[26] Foley, John; Information Week, http://www.informationweek.com/government/cloud-SaaS/how-the-feds-drive-cloud-innovation/240010563

Chapter Three: Big Data 101

"Visualization provides an interesting challenge for computer systems: Data sets are generally quite large, taxing the capacities of main memory, local disk, and even remote disk. We call this the problem of big data."[27]

> \- Michael Cox and David Ellsworth, NASA, 1997
> (describing data from air flow simulations)

What is Big Data?

The most obvious and immediately pertinent fact is that organizations of every type and size are collecting more and more data to improve their decision making. Thus, the linchpin to understanding big data is to understand the intersection of three key elements in a virtuous cycle as depicted in Figure 18: more data, in the data cloud, produces better decisions. Let's begin with the increasing volumes of data:

- "WalMart, a retail giant, handles more than 1m customer transactions every hour, feeding databases estimated at more than 2.5 petabytes..."[28]
- "72 hours of video are uploaded to YouTube every minute"[29]
- 30 billion pieces of content are shared on Facebook every month.[30]

---

[27] Cox, Michael and Ellsworth, David;
Application-controlled demand paging for out-of-core visualization; Proceedings of the 8th conference on Visualization; 1997; Pages 235-ff.
[28] The Economist; Data, data everywhere; Feb 25th 2010;
http://www.economist.com/node/15557443
[29] Youtube Statistics; Press Room; http://www.youtube.com/t/press_statistics
[30] McKinsey Global Institute Report; Big data: The next frontier for innovation, competition, and productivity; May 2011;
http://www.mckinsey.com/insights/mgi/research/technology_and_innovation/big_da ta_the_next_frontier_for_innovation

- The National Climatic Data Center's digital archive, in the last 10 years, experienced a six-fold increase from 1 petabyte to 6 petabytes.[31]

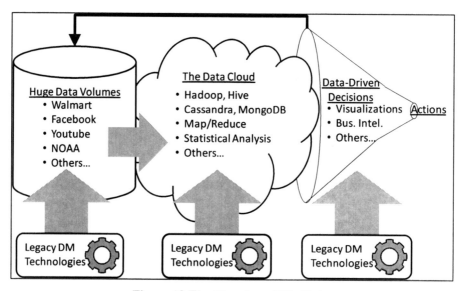

Figure 18 The Meaning of Big Data

As is evident in Figure 18 and the statistics just mentioned, Big Data begins with the central fact that volumes have grown beyond traditional means of processing them in a reasonable time. Besides the increasing volume is the desire by organizations to relate and leverage data from various sources and therefore centralize and integrate the disparate data stores into a single, analyzable store. This was the case and strategy adopted by President Obama's 2012 re-election campaign. The campaign integrated all their disparate databases into a single massive data store they called "Narwhal"[32]. Combine surging volumes with a desire for centralized analysis and you quickly outstrip the

[31] National Climatic Data Center Website; http://www.ncdc.noaa.gov/about-ncdc
[32] Scherer, Michael; Inside the Secret World of the Data Crunchers Who Helped Obama Win; Nov. 07, 2012 ;Time; http://swampland.time.com/2012/11/07/inside-the-secret-world-of-quants-and-data-crunchers-who-helped-obama-win

capabilities of traditional databases. As a final example, consider the data source that really began the big data discussion which is the Google search engine index of all the world's web pages. Clearly such an index of keywords and Universal Resource Locators (URLs) for billions of web pages that needs to return a set of hits in a second or two can neither be stored nor processed on a single computer. Instead, Google turned to massive farms of cheap Linux machines and spread both the index and the search of that index across all of them. Out of that single Google use case sprang the entire ecosystem of big data products, techniques and companies that in Figure 18 we call the "Data cloud". But those techniques would not be experiencing such amazing, exponential growth if they did not have a purpose. For the Obama campaign, their big data efforts enabled them to raise over 1 billion dollars and win the election. In short, big data technologies are providing a return on investment in delivering new insights and enabling better, data-driven decisions. Reminiscent of the W. Edwards Deming quote, "In God we trust, all others must bring data", the demand for decisions based on data, instead of gut instinct, is increasing. Nowadays, partners and customers will assume the data is available to make the right decision; you just need to find a way to get it all, process it in real time and make sense out of it. And that leads us to the third leg of our three-legged big data stool – data-driven decisions for improved decision making. Thomas S. Monson said that "When performance is measured, performance improves."[33] A recent study by the Wharton School of business reports that companies that leverage data-driven decisions achieved 5-6 percent higher productivity than their counterparts.[34] The use of data over intuition has been a business school and boardroom debate for the last several decades; however, the results are now in and

---

[33] Thomas S. Monson. Favorite Quotations from the Collection of Thomas S. Monson. Deseret Books, 1985.
[34] Lohr, Steve; When There's No Such Thing as Too Much Information; NY Times; April 23, 2011; http://www.nytimes.com/2011/04/24/business/24unboxed.html

data-driven decisions have won. Whether it is in the field of baseball (see the book Moneyball[35]), education, evidence-based medicine, or technology; data is winning the debate by improving the decision making. Even before big data, Data Driven Decision Making (D3M) was taking root with the boom in Data Warehouses. Data Warehouses are one of the traditional Data Management technologies depicted feeding into the Big Data components in Figure 18. We will discuss more of these traditional data management techniques in the next section as we examine the history of big data.

History of Big Data

The history of big data is a set of events that weave in and out of different topics to include data management, cloud computing, and business administration. Figure 19 depicts some of the key milestones in the history of big data beginning with one of the earliest examples of automation tackling a huge volume of data.

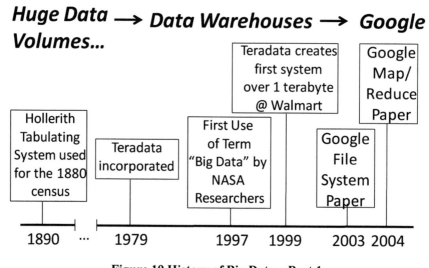

Figure 19 History of Big Data – Part 1

---

[35] Lewis, Michael; Moneyball: The Art of Winning an Unfair Game; ISBN 0-393-05765-8

The United States constitution mandates a decennial census of the population. The first census was taken in 1790. Besides population count, other queries were added to the census and the 1880 census took almost 10 years to publish.[36] In 1890, the census was mechanized using the first electric tabulating system invented by former Census Office employee Herman Hollerith as depicted in Figure 20.

Figure 20 Transcribing Census Data to a Punch Card[37]

The electric tabulating system reduced the census processing time to two and a half years. Also, the total population of 62,622,250 was announced after only six weeks of processing. The reason this is an example of big data is because the size of the data set outgrew the means to efficiently process it and

---

[36] Wikipedia article on the United States Census; http://en.wikipedia.org/wiki/United_States_Census
[37] NARA image in public domain; http://en.wikipedia.org/wiki/File:Card_puncher_-_NARA_-_513295.jpg

therefore a new big data process was necessary in order to accommodate the volume of information. Thus, this represents a physical analogy for the digital history of big data that began with digital record storage on mainframes (for large business) and grew exponentially with the introduction of relational databases in the 1970's. E.F. Codd introduced the relational model in his paper entitled "A Relational Model of Data for Large Shared Data Banks" [38] The evolution of databases bifurcates along the paths of transactional processing (also called On Line Transaction Processing or OLTP) and analytical processing (also called On Line Analytical Processing or OLAP). In relation to Big Data, we are only concerned with the OLAP path as that is the path where you attempt to consolidate an enterprise's data, over time, to mine it and see the patterns and trends in your data. Over time in the 1970's and 1980's, OLAP became more formalized in extracting day-to-day information from the operational systems (performing OLTP, like point of sale systems and inventory systems, etc.; in essence, everything running your business day to day) and loading that into a single large database called a Data Warehouse. Bill Inmon is regarded as the father of Data Warehousing with many books on database design, data warehousing and the Corporate Information Factory (CIF)[39]. Ralph Kimball is another Data Warehouse pioneer that focused more on Data Marts and dimensional modeling (a form of database design). The key point here is that Data Warehousing grew exponentially in the 1990's and matured as a technology with many commercial players with robust Extract, Transform and Load (ETL) tools like Informatica, IBM Infosphere and open source tools like Talend. The commercial presence in data warehousing was felt in the whole packaging and sale of the technology around concepts like business

---

[38] Codd, E.F. (1970). "A Relational Model of Data for Large Shared Data Banks". Communications of the ACM 13 (6): 377–387. http://www.seas.upenn.edu/~zives/03f/cis550/codd.pdf
[39] Inmon, Bill; http://en.wikipedia.org/wiki/Bill_Inmon

intelligence and executive dashboards. As data warehouses grew in volume, traditional approaches around single, expensive database servers could not keep up and data warehouse appliances were born with companies like Terradata and later Netezza (bought by IBM in 2010). As you can see in the timeline (Figure 19), Terradata created the first 1 terabyte parallel processing data warehouse for Walmart in 1999. So, the approach that Terradata and Netezza took to the growth of data warehouses was custom, parallel processing hardware (labeled as an "appliance"). The problem with that type of approach is that it is expensive and only available for a small number of large companies. Enter Google and its challenge of distributing its index of all the world's web pages across thousands of cheap Linux computers. Google solved this problem internally and then posted two whitepapers on their solution in 2003 and 2004 respectively. Those two whitepapers, the first on the Google File System (GFS) and the second on the MapReduce parallel processing algorithm were watershed events in the history of big data for delivering a novel approach to a seemingly intractable problem to solve (without a lot of money). In fact, these two papers are so seminal to the modern big data movement that it is worthwhile for us to delve into their details enough to understand the innovations they introduced. Let's first examine the Google File System as depicted below in Figure 21. A File system is an operating system abstraction where disk space is organized into a system of folders and files that can be read from and written to by application programs. The Google File System is a distributed file system designed to process large, multi-gigabyte files (like log data, weather data, cell phone transactions, etc.) across inexpensive commodity computers in a reasonable amount of time.

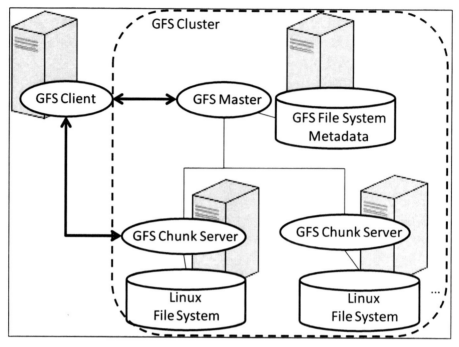

Figure 21 Google File System

Another key assumption for GFS is that hardware failure is expected and therefore seamless recovery and redundancy is built into the file system. GFS accomplishes these benefits by creating a cluster of nodes (called Chunk Servers) controlled by a master node (the master can have backups, called shadow masters, in case it goes down). A "chunk" is the large fixed-size block that all files are decomposed into and kept track of in the file system namespace with other file system metadata managed by the GFS master node. GFS replicates every chunk across three nodes (in case of hardware failure). A GFS client requests a file from the Master Node (which knows what chunks are part of the file and where they are stored). The Master node then instructs the chunk servers to provide the chunks to the client. While GFS is a proprietary system for Google's internal use, its functionality was mimicked in an open source project called Hadoop initiated by Doug Cutting while at Yahoo. Hadoop was named after his son's plush toy elephant. Now let's examine the second Google innovation related to big data, the MapReduce Parallel Processing Framework as depicted below in Figure 22 and which is also part of Hadoop.

MapReduce is a parallel processing framework that involves two stages and a homogeneous data set that can be safely divided into many large chunks (as discussed above in GFS). Figure 22 demonstrates how MapReduce works by examining how it would solve a problem like counting a particular word (or words) in a huge body of text (like all of Wikipedia, or the entire web). The diagram flows from top to bottom and begins with chunks of data dispersed 1 per processing node. On each chunk of data, a mapping function is run to transform the input data into a sequence (or list) of key-value pairs. The concept of a mapping function originated in the Lisp programming language where it allows a function you define to process each element of a list. What you do in your mapping function is unique to your application. In other words, the mapping function is a generic name for your specific instantiation of the function on your specific data. So, when you think of the map function, understand it is a placeholder or container for your unique processing functions – in other words, a black box. The mapping function is a 1:1 operation between input and output. In our example, the map function reads each line of the data, tokenizes it into words and counts of words. The output of this map() function is a key-value pair (k,v), with the key being the word and the value being an integer representing the total # of times (or count) of that word in the chunk of data. Key-value pairs are very important to Big Data in general and NoSQL data stores in particular. "NoSQL" stands for "No Structured Query Language" which is a standard language for using Relational Database Management Systems (RDBMS). So, a NoSQL datastore is a database that is not built upon the relational model. Some NoSQL databases store key-value pairs.

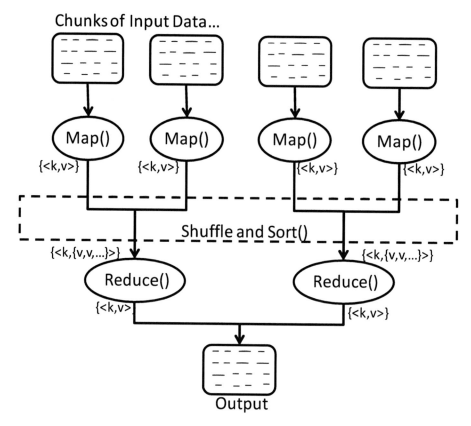

Figure 22 MapReduce Parallel Processing Framework

The reasons Key-Value pairs are so popular are twofold: first, unique keys provide a commonplace and efficient lookup mechanism for the data represented by the key; secondly, the value can be of any type and arbitrarily large affording amazing flexibility and scaling from single values (like an integer) to large binary files (like a video file). Ok, back to our MapReduce example, after mapping our chunks of data into word-count pairs, the pairs are sorted to match up all keys that are the same and then fed to reduce functions. Again, a reduce() function is a generic name for however you want to combine the results for a single key into a single output pair. In the word count example, the reduce function would sum the values to produce a single <word, count> for every word in the input data. The reduce operation can then write the output to an output file. Now we are ready to continue our discussion of the history of big data by moving into the more recent history as depicted in Figure 23.

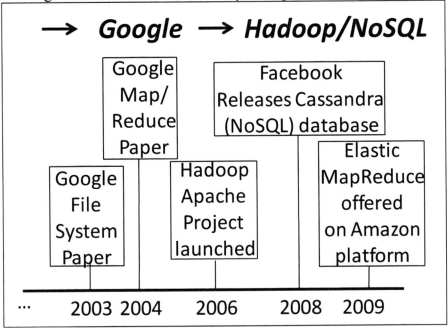

Figure 23 History of Big Data - Part 2

Figure 23 begins with the Google watershed events that we just discussed: GFS and MapReduce. Those events were followed by Doug Cutting working on an open source implementation of those technologies: the Hadoop File System and a MapReduce framework. Together, these are called the Hadoop project. Hadoop has grown considerably into an entire ecosystem of open source projects that we will discuss in the section on Big Data implementations. For now, it is important to understand that most Big Data projects revolve around Hadoop clusters. Besides Hadoop, the other area of explosive growth has been in alternative data storage mechanisms beyond relational database management systems. As mentioned before, these types of data stores are called "NoSQL" databases. While the timeline in Figure 23 only highlights Facebook releasing the

Cassandra NoSQL database in 2008, there are many other NoSQL databases. The similarity between Hadoop and NoSQL databases is that the Hadoop File System is a key-value store just like many of the NoSQL databases. Popular key-value stores are Apache's Cassandra, Amazon's Dynamo DB, Oracle's NoSQL database, Microsoft's Azure Table Storage and many others. Besides key-value stores, there are other types of NoSQL databases like columnar stores, document databases, graph databases, object databases and xml databases. The point here is that huge data volumes are pushing IT vendors and open source developers to innovate and come up with different methods of storing and retrieving large volumes of data. Most of these tools were developed out of necessity because the existing relational database techniques could not scale (without drastically increasing the cost).

The trends revealed in the history of big data are a shift in both hardware and processing techniques to handle the exponentially increasing volumes of data. The hardware trend is a move from singular database servers to massively parallel clusters of computers. The trend in processing techniques is a move from relational technologies to non-relational technologies. Now that we have seen the origins and influences that have shaped this new technology, we are ready to formally define it.

The Definition of Big Data

There are numerous definitions of "Big Data" that focus on different aspects of the problem; however, most of them have enough similarity to elicit a solid understanding of the topic. Let's begin with Wikipedia's definition of big data: "In information technology, big data is a collection of data sets so large and complex that it becomes difficult to process using on-hand database management tools. The challenges include capture, curation, storage, search, sharing, analysis, and visualization."[40] This definition focuses on the problem space, data volumes too large to be processed by conventional methods. Some definitions have expanded upon the problem description to provide more detail on it. Gartner's definition is one of those: "Big data in general is defined as high volume, velocity and variety information assets that demand cost-effective, innovative forms of information processing for enhanced insight and decision making."[41]

The Gartner definition focuses on the 3V's of Big Data: Volume, Velocity and Variety. Let's further define each one of these characteristics of big data:

- **Volume** – the individual size and quantity of data sets in organizations that are increasing exponentially and causing traditional processing techniques to fall short.
- **Velocity** – the speed at which these data sets are coming in is increasing and the speed at which data analysis is required is increasing (requiring more real time analysis). An example of this need is fraud detection where fraud must be recognized and reported to the customer immediately to limit the damage.
- **Variety** – the heterogeneous nature of big data is composed of different types of data to include structured, semi-structured and unstructured data. Types of data include text, audio, video, log data, sensor data, metadata and many others.
- **Other 'V' characteristics** – since the 3 V's have become a popular definition for big data, many people have added new 'V' characteristics to include veracity (data quality and trust), variability (multiple meanings), vulnerability (data security) and value (value to the business). Many pundits call these the "fourth V" of big data.

---

[40] Wikipedia; http://en.wikipedia.org/wiki/Big_data
[41] Gartner IT Glossary; Big Data; http://www.gartner.com/it-glossary/big-data/

The result of all these 'V'-word characteristics amounts to a better understanding of Big Data in relation to the traditional challenges of data management within an organization. In my book, "Information As Product"[42], I examined information management techniques to turn your data into information. Information management is the discipline of cataloging, describing, cleansing, transforming, integrating and analyzing your data assets to produce information for your business units. Shifting the focus of our Big Data definition brings us to how McKinsey Global Institute defined Big Data: "'Big data' refers to datasets whose size is beyond the ability of typical database software tools to capture, store, manage, and analyze."[43] You should notice the shift in emphasis in this definition from the characteristics of big data to the functions of processing the data throughout its lifecycle. This reflects what I stated in the start of this chapter (as is depicted in Figure 18) that legacy data management techniques are an integral part of and influence to the process of leveraging big data. Let's briefly examine each function mentioned in the McKinsey definition:

- **Capture** – the ability for an organization to collect and format the data they wish to analyze. Sometimes this is data in existing operational data stores, or it could be a new data source that they create, or a combination of both.
- **Store** – the ability to persist the data for efficient retrieval and use by applications. In terms of big data, storing the data across numerous processing nodes for efficient, parallel retrieval is critical to delivering acceptable performance.
- **Manage** – data management is a broad area that incorporates numerous sub-processes to include curation,

---

[42] Daconta, Michael; Information As Product: How to deliver the right information, to the right person at the right time; Outskirts Press; © 2007.
[43] James Manyika, Michael Chui, Brad Brown, Jacques Bughin, Richard Dobbs, Charles Roxburgh, Angela Hung Byers; McKinsey Global Institute; Big data: The next frontier for innovation, competition, and productivity; May 2011.

cleansing, cataloging, search, sharing and others. These functions will determine the organization's ability to transform a data source into a valuable data asset that can reliably (and in a repeatable manner) deliver information to the organization. As I covered in detail in my book, Information As Product, the best processes to do this correlate to physical manufacturing processes for creating a physical product. Thus, treating your information (using data as the raw ingredient) like physical products is the best way to deliver business value from those assets.

- **Analyze** – data analysis is the application of a set of techniques to describe, evaluate, understand and extract insights and patterns from data. There are both quantitative and qualitative techniques that are performed. Many techniques involve statistics, logic and other numerical methods. The analysis may or may not include the visualization of the data in order to highlight a pattern, trend or anomaly. Figure 24 demonstrates various visualization techniques applied to different types of data.

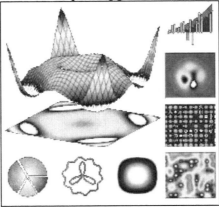

Figure 24 Samples of Data Visualization Techniques to Aid Analysis[44]

---

[44]Image in the Creative Commons by OBACS.
http://commons.wikimedia.org/wiki/File:ScinetChartDataVisualization.PNG

Now that we have examined and explained definitions that focus on different aspects of big data, we can compose a more holistic definition. My definition encapsulates the key ideas from Figure 18 and incorporates elements from the other definitions.

> Big Data is the application of new techniques and platforms to process, analyze and visualize huge volumes of data that are beyond the ability of traditional methods to process in near real time. Some of these techniques leverage cloud computing and create what is called the "data cloud". The purpose of big data is to extract trends, patterns and insights from the data in order to improve organizational decision making. An example of big data is the processing of click stream data on a website, using a Hadoop cluster, to understand customer's buying patterns.

This definition focuses on both the cause and effect of big data on an organization and closes with a clear example. Now that we have a solid definition of Big Data, we can examine how this concept is implemented.

Big Data Implementations and Platforms

As we discussed in the history of Big Data, the most popular and common implementation of Big Data is via the open source project called Hadoop and the numerous products that are layered on top of Hadoop or augment it. Figure 25 depicts the Hadoop ecosystem.

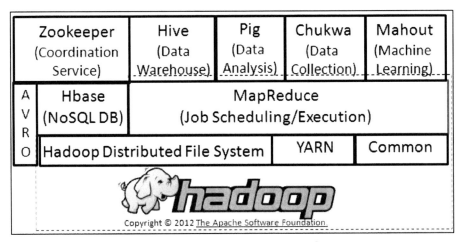

Figure 25 Hadoop Ecosystem[45]

In the Hadoop ecosystem, other apache projects are layered on top of Hadoop or feed into Hadoop (Avro project). Let's examine each component of the diagram in detail:

- Hadoop – the base system is composed of core components that provide distributed processing and storage.
  - Hadoop Distributed File System (HDFS) – open source software modeled after the Google File System that enables the processing of very large files across hundreds or thousands of compute nodes.
  - MapReduce – open source version of Google's MapReduce that provides a parallel processing framework for manipulating huge volumes of homogenous data. The most recent version has been re-engineered to use the YARN framework (see below).

---

[45] Note: this is only a partial view of the ecosystem, there are many more open source and commercial projects that leverage hadoop. Additionally, Hadoop ® logo used with permission under the Apache license per http://www.apache.org/foundation/marks/

- o <u>Hadoop Common</u> – a set of utilities used across multiple hadoop projects.
- o <u>Hadoop YARN</u> – a generic job scheduling and tracking framework for distributed processing.
- <u>Avro</u> – a data serialization framework based on the JavaScript Object Notation (JSON) used to either communicate between Hadoop nodes or for persistent data storage. It can also be used for client programs to send data to Hadoop services.
- <u>HBase</u> – a NoSQL type database (called a "column-oriented" store) that can be used to provide random, realtime read/write access to your Big Data. This is in contrast to HDFS which is optimized for mostly read access of large files. HBase is an open source implementation of Google's Bigtable, which was also described in a published paper[46].
- <u>Hive</u> – a data warehouse system built on top of Hadoop that provides an SQL-like language called HiveQL for the analysis of large datasets. There are tools in the project to perform Extract, Transform and Load (ETL) of external data sources into Hive. Additionally, it provides an SQL-like syntax to query and analyze large data sets. Finally, it allows programmers to also leverage MapReduce and plugin custom mappers and reducers for more sophisticated analysis.
- <u>Pig</u> – a data analysis language (called Pig Latin) that can load, transform and store data for use in Hadoop MapReduce jobs. These commands can be stored in Pig scripts and even run in MapReduce mode. The Getting Started tutorial demonstrates how to use Pig Latin to

---

[46] Fay Chang, Jeffrey Dean, Sanjay Ghemawat, Wilson C. Hsieh, Deborah A. Wallach, Mike Burrows, Tushar Chandra, Andrew Fikes, and Robert E. Gruber; <u>Bigtable: A Distributed Storage System for Unstructured Data</u>; http://research.google.com/archive/bigtable.html

determine the frequency of a phrase in a body of text (similar to our word count example described above).

- Chukwa – a data collection system for monitoring large distributed systems built on top of HBase, HDFS and MapReduce. Chukwa writes its data to HBase via agent processes that collect and send data to the collector process. The Hadoop Infrastructure Care Center (HICC) is the Chukwa web user interface that acts as the console.

- Mahout – a machine learning library that leverages Hadoop. As of the time of publication, Mahout supports four use cases: recommendation mining which suggests new items to users from examining user's behavior; clustering which takes text documents and groups them into statistically related topics; classification which learns from existing categorized documents what documents of a category look like so as to assign new documents to the correct category; and frequent item set mining which takes a set of item groups and identifies which individual items usually appear together.

- Zookeeper – a distributed coordination system through a shared hierarchical namespace of data registers (similar to a file system but called znodes). Zookeeper is designed to efficiently store coordination data like status information, configuration and location information. Clients connect to zookeeper via a TCP connection to send requests, get responses, get watch events and send "heartbeats" (which are "I'm alive" messages). For example, Hbase uses Zookeeper to coordinate amongst its distributed servers and hold distributed configuration information.

As should be evident from the numerous systems described above, Apache Hadoop is a thriving ecosystem that is continually growing and improving. There are even commercial vendors that package and support Hadoop distributions like Cloudera. Other vendors, like MapR, have extended Hadoop with enterprise features like recovery, snapshots and mirroring. So, while most IT professionals consider use of Hadoop to be the primary tool for Big Data implementations (as it involves both storage and processing of big data), some use the term more as an umbrella category that includes the use of NoSQL data stores in an organization (which only focus on storage and retrieval of "big data"). Now let's examine how NoSQL data stores are being used to store and access huge volumes of data.

As mentioned in the History of Big Data chapter, NoSQL stands for "No Structured Query Language" data stores (note that some people have modified the name to mean "Not Only" SQL), in contrast to traditional database management systems that leverage the SQL language for query and table manipulation. All NoSQL data stores share the common driver of handling huge volumes of data in a manner that is simpler and easier than the technique of "sharding" a database to handle huge volumes. Sharding a database is the act of partitioning a database by rows (also called "horizontal partitioning") across multiple servers. In other words, a large database is split into multiple smaller databases (with the same structure) on multiple servers. This has the advantage of improved performance as the tables on each shard are smaller; however, it comes with book-keeping complexity to manage the multiple shards consistently and is not suitable for all types of data (especially if a query needs to cross shards). How you shard data is often very dependent on the data itself; for example, is it best to separate the data by time or by geography? So, in lieu of sharding, the NoSQL community focuses on other techniques to store data. Here are the major types of NoSQL stores:

- Key/Value stores – a distributed storage mechanism that stores data in a "schema-less" way as a set of key-value pairs. By "schema-less" we mean that the data does not follow a structure or model like an entity-relationship model in a database or an object-oriented model in programming. Software programmers are very familiar with storing key-value pairs as there are several common data structures (like hash tables) that can store this type of data. Figure 26 depicts a Hash Table.

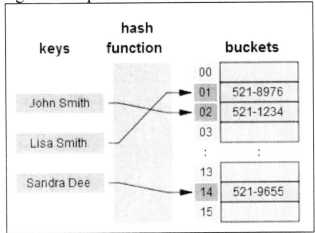

Figure 26 Hash Table Stores Key-Value Pairs[47]

In Figure 26, we see a set of keys (full names on the left) that are mapped to values stored in the array. The mapping process is done via a one-way hash function that transforms the key into an index in the array. If the "bucket space" or array is small, two keys can hash to the same index and therefore a collision scheme is necessary to handle two keys that point to the same index. Usually, a simple method like allowing a bucket to hold a list of items can resolve hash clashes. Many vendors including Amazon, Oracle, and multiple open source projects have taken this basic key-value pair data model and implemented robust NoSQL data stores that are highly scalable and very fast for key-based retrieval of data.

- Column stores – whereas a traditional relational database management system (RDBMS) stores data in rows (where each entity is stored as a single row); column stores

---

[47] Diagram by Jorge Stolfi and published in the public domain; http://en.wikipedia.org/wiki/File:Hash_table_3_1_1_0_1_0_0_SP.svg

partition the data vertically by column (or field). A simple example can demonstrate the difference. Let's say we have a Person record with five fields: id, first name, last name, birth date and birth country. Storing two rows of data would look like this:

- o 1, Joe, Smith, 1/3/1955, USA
- o 2, Sally, Smith, 4/14/1972, England

That same data stored as columns would be:

- o 1,2
- o Joe, Sally
- o Smith, Smith
- o 1/3/1955, 4/14/1972
- o USA, England

There are advantages to column stores especially for very wide tables where only a small number of columns need to be returned in response to a query. Open source projects like Cassandra (mentioned in the History of Big Data) are based on column storage.

- Graph stores – a graph is a data structure designed to store data as a set of connected, or linked, nodes as depicted in Figure 27.

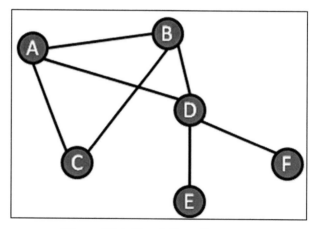

Figure 27 A Graph Data Structure

We will see this graph structure again, in detail, in the next chapter on Linked Data. Just like our key-value pairs, graph structures are very common data structures in computer science and familiar to every programmer. HyperText Markup Language (HTML) documents and eXtensible Markup Language (XML) documents are represented as a graph as depicted in Figure 28. It is important to understand that a tree is a type of graph where nodes have non-cyclical links.

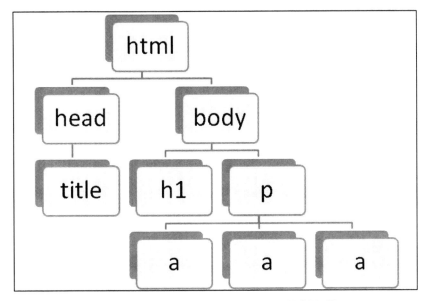

Figure 28 An HTML Document Object Model (DOM) Tree

A graph store, or graph database, is optimized to store these types of structures and especially web documents (XML and HTML). A flat graph, a parent with a single set of children, can be used to mimic a relational table so these graph stores can also store traditional entities (like Customer, Product, etc.)

- <u>Document stores</u> – this type of data store uses the "document" as its base model and is optimized for the storage and retrieval of documents. These data stores focus on what is called unstructured or semi-structured data which accounts for between 70-80% of all data in organizations[48].

At this point in our survey of implementation tools for Big Data, we have covered the Hadoop ecosystem and NoSQL Databases. Now, it is time we examine the third leg of our stool: data management tools that focus on the preparation, quality and management of big data stores. All the major data management tool vendors like IBM's Infosphere, CloverETL, Informatica, Talend, Splunk and Pentaho (to name a few), all offer integration with Hadoop. Most of the data integration tools follow a common look and feel where they present a palette to the user for creating a data flow diagram as depicted in Figure 29 below.

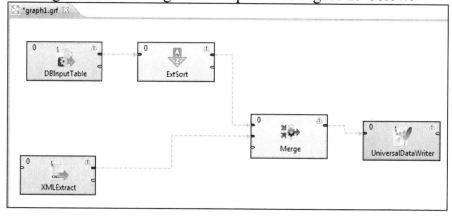

Figure 29 Data Quality and Integration Tools Palette[49]

---

[48] "Unstructured Data and the 80 Percent Rule"; Seth Grimes; © 2011 Clarabridge; http://clarabridge.com/default.aspx?tabid=137&ModuleID=635&ArticleID=551

[49] CloverETL Designer; http://www.cloveretl.com/products/desktop-edition

Now we can move on from implementation tools to the people that know how to use them – data scientists. The critical role of a data scientist in your big data initiatives cannot be overstated.

Role of the Data Scientist

More important than the platforms used for Big Data are the people with the necessary skills to statistically analyze, manipulate, make sense out of and visualize your data to derive business insights and values out of those massive data stores. These people are called data scientists and are highly sought after. Proof of this high demand is Walmart's recruiting effort as depicted by the photo in Figure 30.

Figure 30 Walmart Big Data Recruitment Billboard[50]

---

[50] Photo by Sicular, Svetlana and Gartner; June 22, 2012; Used with permission; http://blogs.gartner.com/svetlana-sicular/the-data-is-big-literally/

Figure 30 depicts a large Walmart recruitment sign off highway 101 near Redwood City, California. Data scientists are those talented people that can find meaning, sometimes hidden meaning, in your data using the techniques of statistics, data mining and predictive analytics. More important than the tools discussed above are the people that know how to use those tools. I cannot stress enough the fact that you cannot have a big data program without recruiting people with these skills.

Let's examine the type of problem that a data scientist solves to deliver value to your organization. In the book (and movie) "Moneyball" we see the General Manager rely upon his data scientist, Peter Brand (aka Paul DePodesta), to use data to find undervalued players with key characteristics they want. For example, the Oakland A's General Manager, Billy Beane, was able to use statistics to see the value of catcher Scott Hatteberg even after he injured his throwing arm[51]. After the injury, Hatteberg became a free agent and no team wanted him because a catcher that cannot throw is not effective; however, Billy Beane was more interested in Hatteberg's statistics as a hitter where his on-base percentage and pitches per plate appearance were far above the average. So, because of carefully watching the statistics, the Oakland Athletics valued Scott Hatteberg as a hitter when every other team only saw him as a catcher. This example shows how a data scientist can leverage data and statistical analysis to draw out non-intuitive insights from the evidence.

Recently, a new online crowdsourcing platform has emerged for the Data Science community called Kaggle and available at Kaggle.com. Kaggle's website has three components: a competition platform that challenges and ranks the best data scientists, a marketplace to connect companies to the best data scientists, and a Workbench of tools that are available by project or on a subscription basis.

---

[51] National Public Radio; "'Moneyball': Tracking Down How Stats Win Games"; September 23, 2011; http://www.npr.org/2011/09/23/140703403/moneyball-tracking-down-how-stats-win-games

Kaggle boasts over 87,000 data scientists and is a potentially disruptive force[52] in the labor market for data scientists because it eliminates the problem of geography in finding and attracting the best talent for your data science problems. Kaggle.com also ranks the competitors and a data scientist's "Kaggle Ranking" has become a requirement for some job listings at large companies. So, Kaggle.com is an interesting new development from both the consumer side (employers) and the producer side (data scientists) that may be able to help you with your big data challenges.

Big Data Case Study

The Obama reelection campaign of 2012 raised over 1 billion dollars and won the election in part due to a sophisticated team of data scientists that used big data analytics in the Amazon cloud. Although many of the details have been kept secret, there is enough public information on their strategy to understand their basic techniques and to gain insights into their success. First, in terms of background, there is the business perspective or the need for a new approach and then there is the technical implementation perspective. Let's begin with the business perspective: the Obama campaign's approach to the 2012 election was to reassemble the coalition that elected the President in 2008 with the added difficulty of the stunning loss in the 2010 elections. To reassemble the coalition meant to assemble the various factions for multiple purposes to include fundraising, volunteering, getting out the vote and voting for the President. To accomplish this meant taking their data on that coalition to a new level of granularity, being able to process it in multiple ways for different purposes, develop a model of each voter, and through experimentation attempt to influence that voter (or get

---

[52] Goetz, Thomas; "How Kaggle Is Changing How We Work"; April 12, 2013; The Atlantic; http://www.theatlantic.com/technology/archive/2013/04/how-kaggle-is-changing-how-we-work/274908/

them to act) by targeting what matters to them. Let's now examine the key technological innovations that led to this triumph in the use of Big Data:

- <u>Project Narwhal</u> – the Obama technical team first consolidated multiple databases ("silos") into a single data store as depicted in Figure 31.

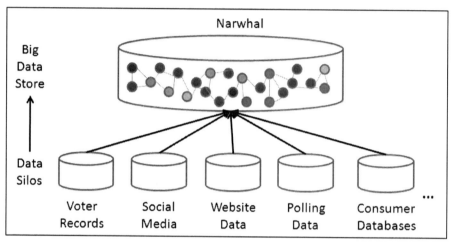

Figure 31 "Narwhal" Big Data Store Consolidates Silos

Not only did this consolidate all the data on voters and their interactions with the campaign in one place, it also was accessed through a single services-based Application Programming Interface (the Narwhal API). From the business perspective, the campaign was able to get a 360 degree view of every voter they were trying to target. This unprecedented level of granularity went far beyond demographic slices down to what would it take to move individual voters to get the results they wanted. From the technical perspective, this created a huge volume of data accessible to every application the campaign would create with only a single source of truth so that every application always had the right information. It is this same bold move that many businesses and Government organizations need to do with their disparate data silos. This great cloud migration offers the best chance yet to finally consolidate your organization's data. In fact, from the technical perspective, the Obama campaign leveraged the cloud to enable this solution by implementing Narwhal using the Amazon Relational Database Service (RDS) for storage and the Amazon Simple Queue Service (SQS) to integrate data from providers into the database. For the campaign application, Narwhal exposed a simple REST-based (REST stands for Representational State Transfer and means that the API leverages the same protocols that web browsers and servers use) and language-neutral API. "The resulting platform gave Obama for America tools that helped 'force-multiply' volunteers, giving them organizational and communication tools that made the Obama 'ground game' even more effective."[53]

- The fine-grained Voter Model – in reassembling the coalition that elected the President in 2008, the goal was to address the voters as individuals and connect them to all their interactions with the campaign and all the information about them from various sources. This fine-grained model of each voter also included four scores: the likelihood to vote, the likelihood to be an Obama supporter, likelihood of being an Obama donor (or volunteer), and the likelihood of being persuaded by a particular topic. Each of these scores were measured and modified after each interaction with the candidate and that was how the campaign would micro-target voters for promotions. One important lesson learned from this model is that it leverages techniques we will be discussing

---

[53] Gallagher, Sean; "Built to win: Deep inside Obama's campaign tech";November 14, 2012; http://arstechnica.com/information-technology/2012/11/built-to-win-deep-inside-obamas-campaign-tech/

in the Linked Data chapter.

- <u>Thousands of Experiments and Simulations</u> – on top of connecting the data and scoring the voters, the campaign ran their own polls, crafted experiments to influence particular voters and ran simulations of the election for each state. Let's examine each of these tactics in detail. Instead of relying on the national polls, the Obama campaign augmented state polling with their own efforts to do live surveys of voters to identify Obama supporters. "In September and October, the campaign completed 8,000 to 9,000 calls per night."[54] Additionally, the Obama campaign would craft multiple versions of emails to test variations of subject lines, amount of money to ask for and topics. This is called A-B testing where they count the response on two different variations to determine which is more effective and then go with the more effective version on a wider audience. In June, a "blockbuster" fundraising line emerged from this testing process with a subject of "I will be outspent"[55]. Finally, the campaign was also able to leverage the data in running simulations to predict the outcome of the election in the battleground states. "'We ran the election 66,000 times every night,' said a senior official, describing the computer simulations the campaign ran to figure out Obama's odds of winning each swing state. 'And every morning we got the spit-out — here are your chances of winning these states. And that is how we allocated

---

[54] Blumenthal, Mark; Obama Campaign Polls: How The Internal Data Got It Right; 11/21/2012; http://www.huffingtonpost.com/2012/11/21/obama-campaign-polls-2012_n_2171242.html

[55] Green, Joshua; The Science Behind Those Obama Campaign E-Mails; 11/29/2012; http://www.businessweek.com/articles/2012-11-29/the-science-behind-those-obama-campaign-e-mails

resources.'"[56]

- <u>Micro-targeting voters</u> – all of the previous items were building a platform that enabled easy micro-targeting of voters in order to reassemble the Obama coalition. By micro-targeting we mean selecting a thin slice of the electorate that responds to a particular issue and then target those voters with experiments and promotions. Examples of this abound in the re-election to include the President participating in a Reddit forum to target the youth vote, the administration creating a policy not to deport young illegal immigrants, the President changing his position on gay marriage and many others. Other examples of micro-targeting involve a system to leverage the TV viewing habits of specific voters to micro-target them with messages and the sending of multiple different versions of emails to different groups. The campaign's micro-targeting effort proved effective in persuading some voters.

Now, let's put together all the pieces we discussed and examine the Obama campaign's Big Data architecture in its totality as depicted below in Figure 32. The big data architecture depicted in Figure 32 is a Cloud architecture that leverages Amazon Web Services (AWS) Infrastructure-as-a Service offerings. It is also a Service-Oriented Architecture (SOA) because the applications communicate via simple REST-based services (REST is an acronym for Representational State Transfer that uses the same protocol as the World Wide Web). Another key item in the Obama Big Data Architecture is the separation of applications from the data and the elimination of data silos. Data and Information Management professionals have warned of the dangers of data silos for years and taught organizations how to

---

[56] Scherer, Michael; How Obama's data crunchers helped him win; 11/8/2012; Time; http://www.cnn.com/2012/11/07/tech/web/obama-campaign-tech-team/index.html

use data integration and information management to overcome them.

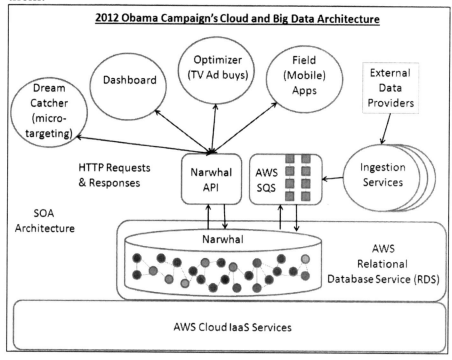

Figure 32 Obama Campaign Big Data Architecture

The Obama campaign took an even bolder approach that leveraged the scalability of the cloud to consolidate those data silos into a single data store. Effectively, this created a separate "data layer" in the architecture that could be leveraged by the "business logic layer." This clean separation shows both modularity and loose coupling and is an excellent design principle. Finally, the fine-grained and statistics-based voter model was an innovation in terms of fidelity, linking data together and providing a 360 degree view of a voter (i.e. who last interacted with this voter?). Linking data items (also called nodes) together in order to more fully understand them is a technique being leveraged widely in social networks like Facebook and Google plus and is the topic of our next chapter.

Chapter Four: Linked Data 101

"The technology is linked data, and it's extremely simple. If you want to put something on the web there are three rules: first thing is that those HTTP names — those things that start with "http:" — we're using them not just for documents now, we're using them for things that the documents are about. ...

Second rule, if I take one of these HTTP names and I look it up and I do the web thing with it and I fetch the data using the HTTP protocol from the web, I will get back some data in a standard format which is kind of useful data that somebody might like to know about that thing, about that event. ...

Third rule is that when I get back that information it's not just got somebody's height and weight and when they were born, it's got relationships. Data is relationships. Interestingly, data is relationships. This person was born in Berlin, Berlin is [in] Germany."

- Sir Tim Berners-Lee
TED Talk in 2009[57]

What is Linked Data?

Linked data is a particular method for publishing information on the World Wide Web that ensures it is machine readable, connected to other information, and exposes its meaning (also known as "semantics"). It is a small part of a larger vision proposed by Sir Tim Berners-Lee, the creator of the World Wide Web. The larger vision espoused by Berners-Lee is called the "Semantic Web" and is a web of machine-readable (vice human-readable) content. The current web can only be processed by humans as it is composed of specially formatted text called the Hyper-Text Markup Language (HTML) which is basically formatted text with links (called hyperlinks) to other

---

[57] Tim Berners Lee; TED2009 Talk;
http://www.ted.com/talks/tim_berners_lee_on_the_next_web.html

bodies of text. Hyperlinks are the key characteristic that makes the World Wide Web an actual web (aka graph) where documents are connected to other documents as depicted in Figure 33.

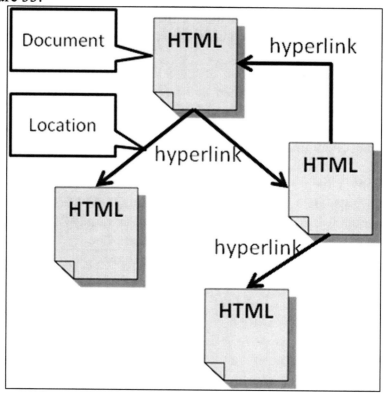

Figure 33 The Graph (Web) Structure of the World Wide Web

Figure 33 demonstrates that the computer web is a set of connected, human readable documents. The links between documents are called hyperlinks and they do three things: first, they create a section of text in the current document that becomes highlighted (usually underlined) and denoted as "clickable" in the browser; second, the link specifies the physical location on the web where another HTML document exists; third, the link specifies the protocol the web browser should use to go and fetch the document at the other end of the link (typically this is the HTTP protocol which stands for "hyper-text transfer protocol").

Figure 34 depicts a hyperlink in a browser and its corresponding HTML. It cannot be understated how important those hyperlinks, also called Universal Resource Locators (URLs), are to the current web, the semantic web and Linked Data (as highlighted in the opening quote of the chapter).

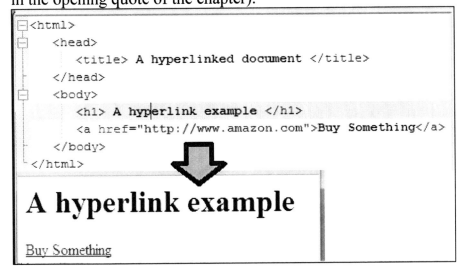

Figure 34 An Example of an HTML Hyperlink (aka URL)

In Figure 34 we see two views of the same thing. The top view is the actual HTML tags that are interpreted by the browser to render the page shown in the bottom view. The link in the bottom view (the underlined words "Buy Something") is clickable and will go and fetch the "default page" from the Amazon.com website. A link is created via the anchor tag (represented in HTML by the single letter 'a' and the href attribute which provides the location of the remote resource. The href actually has two parts separated by a colon: the first part is the communication protocol the web browser should use to fetch the resource and the second part is the location of the resource (which uses both a domain name of the server and optionally an additional directory structure). In the case of Figure 34, only a domain name is used which means that the web server at that location will be asked for a "default page" which is usually index.html (but that can be set in the web server). Ok, now that we drilled down into the details of the current web, let's pull back up to the big picture and understand what Mr. Berners-Lee created with the current web and how he hopes to evolve those concepts to a more semantic-based web. The current web exposes documents to people but has no way of representing the knowledge in those documents to machines. That is why we say the current way is "human-readable" and not "machine-readable". Machines, in particular computers, are not very good at understanding and interpreting the meaning of natural language even though this is the subject of a lot of active research. Given that understanding natural language is hard, can we represent our information on the web in a manner that better represents the knowledge in the data (what it is, how it can be applied) by machines so that those machines can execute actions on your behalf? For example, could a doctor's website represent their available appointments on the web in such a way that an intelligent software agent that understands your schedule (also represented on the web) could arbitrate with the doctor's software agent to schedule an appointment time that fits your schedule? If that data of available appointments and your schedule could be represented in a way that the knowledge contained in that data (what is an event? What is an activity? What is a daily schedule? How does travel time affect scheduling activities? etc.) could be exposed to an intelligent software agent, then the web would move beyond presenting data to humans to presenting data to other computers acting on our behalf. In fact, it is important to understand that Apple's Siri technology leverages many of these same semantic techniques to perform its actions as an intelligent assistant. Siri has models of what concepts like a "Restaurant" are and what it should do related to a restaurant like "make a reservation". Let's complete this rather technical discussion by coming back to our notion of hyperlinks and how they are used in linked data. The key insight and use of the URL is to use them for more than the location of a document and instead use them to refer to a particular concept that you want to talk about. For example, if I want to talk about a "hospital", I could use a URL that points to data that explains what I mean by the term hospital. This gives me two significant benefits in knowledge representation: first, it gives me a simple, comfortable way to represent the unique identity of a concept; and secondly, it gives me a simple method of storing retrievable data (like the attributes of a hospital, its definition, its purpose, activities you do at hospitals, etc.) at that location. So, in a nutshell, we have evolved the concept of a URL from a document location to a unique identity for a concept we know about. And, even more importantly, we shared this knowledge on the web in an open format. This is happening today, as depicted in Figure 35, and what is referred to as "Linked Open Data".

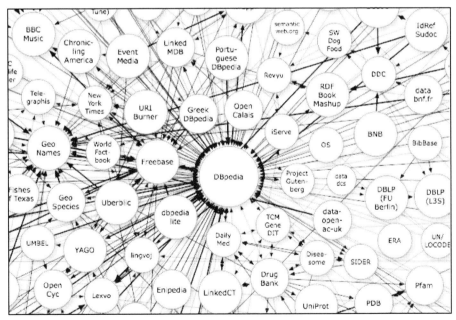

Figure 35 The Linked Open Data Cloud (LOD) Diagram[58]

Figure 35 depicts stores of linked open data that leverage each

---

[58] A portion of the Creative Commons Image map at http://lod-cloud.net/ by Richard Cyganiak and Anja Jentzsch.

other's knowledge representation (depicted via the links between sites). It should be evident than many sites are representing knowledge and referring to concepts in other sites. The circle at the center is called DBPedia[59] and is a linked data version of Wikipedia. Figure 36 depicts a snippet of the DBPedia entry for the German City of Berlin.

About: <u>Berlin</u>

An Entity of Type : <u>populated place</u>, from Named Graph : <u>http://dbpedia.org</u>, within Data Space : <u>dbpedia.org</u>

Berlin is the capital city of Germany and one of the 16 states of Germany. With a population of 3.5 million people, Berlin is Germany's largest city and is the second most populous city proper and the eighth most populous urban area in the European Union. Located in northeastern Germany, it is the center of the Berlin-Brandenburg Metropolitan Region, which has 5.9 million residents from over 190 nations. Located in the European Plains, Berlin is influenced by a temperate seasonal climate.

Property	Value
dbpedia-owl:PopulatedPlace/areaTotal	• 891.85
dbpedia-owl:abstract	• Berlin is the capital city of Germany and one of the 16 state people, Berlin is Germany's largest city and is the second populous urban area in the European Union. Located in norl •••
dbpedia-owl:areaCode	• 030
dbpedia-owl:areaTotal	• 891850000.000000 (xsd:double)
dbpedia-owl:country	• dbpedia:Germany
dbpedia-owl:elevation	• 34.000000 (xsd:double)

Figure 36 DBpedia Entry (Partial) for Berlin

Now, let's examine another snippet of the same data in the "raw" format depicted below in Figure 37:

```
<rdf:Description rdf:about="http://dbpedia.org/resource/Berlin">
    <rdf:type rdf:resource="http://dbpedia.org/class/yago/StatesOfGermany"/>
    <rdf:type rdf:resource="http://www.w3.org/2002/07/owl#Thing"/>
    <rdf:type rdf:resource="http://dbpedia.org/ontology/Place"/>
...
    <owl:sameAs rdf:resource="http://es.dbpedia.org/resource/Berlin"/>
    <owl:sameAs rdf:resource="http://pt.dbpedia.org/resource/Berlim"/>
...
    <foaf:homepage rdf:resource="http://www.berlin.de/international/index.en.php"/>
...
    <geo:lat rdf:datatype="http://www.w3.org/2001/XMLSchema#float">52.5006</geo:lat>
    <geo:long rdf:datatype="http://www.w3.org/2001/XMLSchema#float">13.3989</geo:long>
    <dbpprop:name xml:lang="en">Berlin</dbpprop:name>
```

Figure 37 Raw Data for DBpedia Entry of Berlin

While the raw data may not seem familiar, it actually follows a

---

[59]DBPedia is in the Creative Commons. http://wiki.dbpedia.org/About

simple pattern modeled after an English sentence by having a Subject, a Predicate and an Object. In Figure 37, the first Subject is the rdf:about reference with a URL for Berlin, the Predicate is the rdf:type tag and the Object is a "State Of Germany". In other words, this is capturing the knowledge that Berlin is a State of Germany. The statements below it capture the knowledge that Berlin is a type of Thing and a type of Place. This generic knowledge becomes very important when you are trying to reason about groups of things. Figure 38 depicts the common structure used for Linked Data in graphical form.

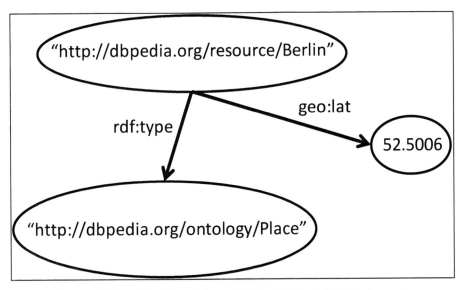

Figure 38 Graphical Depiction of Linked Data S-P-O Statements

In examining Figure 38, it is first important to remember our discussion about identity and the use of URLs for concepts (like Berlin). You may be asking, "Why not just use the single word 'Berlin' like we do in natural language?" The problem with single word labels is that they are rarely unique and they are often ambiguous and not the only single word used to represent the concept. Thus, using a URL gives us a unique way of identifying the concept and then you can attach any number of single word labels as you like to the uniquely identified things in order to make matching on it (or discovering it) easier. So, the subject is the unique URL for the city of Berlin. There are two predicates shown in our diagram and they are rdf:type and geo:lat. The predicate "rdf:type" represents a type of another concept also known as an "IS-A" predicate (for example, Berlin 'IS A' place). The predicate "geo:lat" represents the geographic latitude of the city. Thus, you can see the difference in objects in the diagram whereas the rdf:type predicate points to another concept (represented by a URL for the concept 'Place') and the geo:lat predicate points to a literal number (52.5006). This simple Subject, Predicate and Object (S,P,O) pattern is a very powerful model that can represent a wide variety of knowledge. Additionally, it should be evident that these S,P,O triples can continually be connected and pointed to by other triples in a large, connected graph (or web) of knowledge. Even a world-wide web of knowledge! Now, I hope you are starting to see how Tim Berners-Lee's vision involves moving from sharing documents via the web to sharing knowledge via the web.

Tim Berner-Lee's vision of the semantic web and the W3C standardization process for the semantic web has been around for over a decade before linked data became popular. In fact, interest in the semantic web has waxed and waned over the years partly due to a chicken and egg problem between a lack of standards and/or lack of good data stores that use the standards. In many ways, the push for linked data is one way to break the logjam of semantically rich data to fuel the next generation of semantically-enabled applications. Besides the format, the use of linked data is also related to the rise of popular websites like MySpace, Facebook and Google+. These sites create and manage your "social graph" as depicted in Figure 39. In its simplest form a social graph connects you to the people you know or, in terms popularized by Facebook,[60] to your "friends" and "friends of friends".

---

[60] http://www.facebook.com/

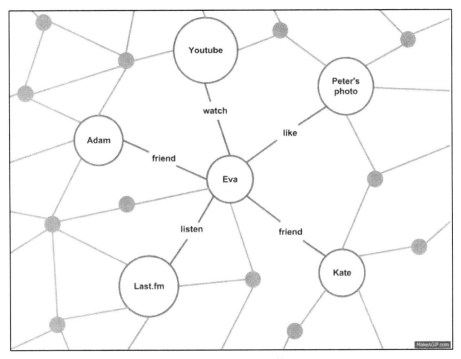

Figure 39 A Social Graph[61] for Eva

Figure 39 depicts a social graph of a fictitious girl named "Eva". The nodes in the graph, represented via circles, are the "nouns" or things that can be connected like other people, artifacts on the web (like an image) and websites like YouTube and Last.fm. The links are usually verbs including the word "friend" which has become a verb (much in the same way that google has become a verb). You could read "friend" to mean "create a friend connection". What Tim Berners Lee realized and leveraged was the fact that the Semantic Web already had the facility to create a social graph (for example, projects like Friend-of-a-Friend, FOAF, pre-date Facebook). Thus, you could argue that linked data is the semantic web hopping on the social graph bandwagon. At the same time, one other key event was taking shape that would influence linked data – Government

---

[61] A creative commons image by user: Festys at
http://en.wikipedia.org/wiki/File:Social_graph.gif

transparency. We will examine the influence of that in our discussion of the history of linked data in the next section.

The History of Linked Data

The history of linked data is truly a history of intersections between three powerful movements. Figure 40 depicts a timeline of the key events in that history.

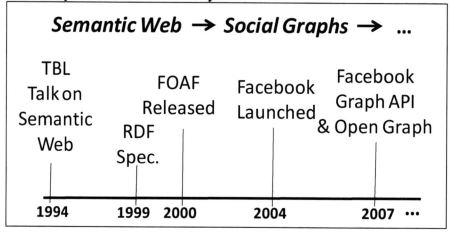

Figure 40 The Linked Data Timeline Part 1

Figure 40 begins in 1994 when Tim Berners-Lee, at the first World Wide Web conference, discussed the need for a Semantic Web of data. Strictly speaking, we could go back further if we want to examine the long history of knowledge representation that forms the underpinnings of the Semantic web and began with Aristotle. Instead, we will cover linked data in its relation to the World Wide Web and the semantic web as those two contributions by Tim Berners-Lee form the foundation of all aspects of Linked Data and are driving its evolution. In 1999, Tim Berners-Lee's vision of the Semantic Web began to materialize in the form of a data format, entitled the Resource Description Framework (RDF), that was depicted above in Figures 39 and 40 (the "raw" DBPedia data). One key use of

RDF was the Friend-of-a-Friend (FOAF[62]) format. If you want to see what FOAF looks like, you can use a web application called FOAF-a-matic[63] to generate a FOAF file on yourself. An interesting point about FOAF is that it connects people using the relationship "knows". So, you could describe attributes about yourself (name, email, homepage, etc.) and then link to other people via the "foaf:knows" relationship. For example, Mike knows Lynne. In terms of the timeline, FOAF was creating a social graph before Facebook existed. Facebook was created by Mark Zuckerberg while attending Harvard University and was launched in February 2004. Much more than a data format, Facebook popularized the notion of the social graph in the same way that the graphical web browser popularized the internet. In fact, it is important to note that in terms of adoption, RDF and FOAF cannot compare with the meteoric rise of Facebook and other social networking sites. Additionally, while Facebook is the most popular social networking website, it was not the first or the only one. MySpace launched in 2003 and Orkut is a popular social networking site in India and Brazil. The key point here is that the phenomena of social networking grew out of the management of a simple data graph on people and their relationships to other people and things (like images, music, sites they like, etc.) In terms of the evolution of the web, we see a group of web applications following Tim Berner-Lee's vision of moving beyond documents to knowledge (in this case, knowledge about your relationships). Facebook has created a development platform around their social graph to enable third party developers to access it and extend it. To accomplish this, Facebook created and published a Graph API to allow third party developers to read and write data to Facebook (once properly authenticated). The Facebook API uses the existing social graph but does not change that graph. To extend the graph to new actions and objects, Facebook created "Open Graph" and the

---

[62] http://www.foaf-project.org/
[63] http://www.ldodds.com/foaf/foaf-a-matic

"Open Graph Protocol". Open Graph enables Facebook third party applications to create new verbs and objects to extend Facebook's Social Graph. On the Facebook developer site, they show an example of creating a new application that adds the verb "Cook" and a new "Recipe" object to the facebook open graph. The Open Graph Protocol [64] (OGP) enables any website to become part of Facebook's open graph by adding a set of "<Meta>" tags to the header of its HTML page. The types of objects that can be pointed to by the Open Graph Protocol are music, video, website, article, book and profile. The Open Graph Protocol follows Tim Berners-Lee's vision of using URLs to identify concepts. For example, here is the unique URL to refer to a video: http://ogp.me/ns/video# . Now, let's move on to the next watershed event in the history of linked data – open government data as depicted in Figure 41.

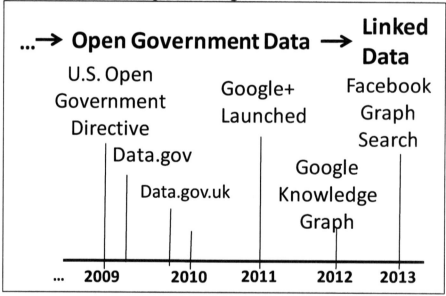

Figure 41 History of Linked Data Part 2

As depicted in Figure 41, on January 20, 2009, President Barack Obama released a Memorandum on "Transparency and Open

---

[64] http://ogp.me/

Government" that laid out the principles of a transparent, participatory and collaborative Government. This memorandum gave the Office of Management and Budget (OMB) 120 days to create a directive on how agencies should fulfill the spirit of the memorandum. On December 8, 2009, OMB released the Open Government Directive to all U.S. Federal Departments and Agencies requiring them to create a gateway http://www.[agency].gov/open on their public-facing websites; to publish three high-value datasets to http://www.data.gov, and create an Open Government plan for public review on how they will implement transparency into their processes. I assisted the government team working on data.gov to produce a Concept of Operations[65] document for the site and solely drafted the section on integrating Semantic Web concepts into the site. The data.gov portal is depicted in Figure 42.

Figure 42 Data.gov[66]

---

[65] http://ideascale.com/userimages/sub-1/736312/ConOpsFinal.pdf
[66] The data.gov site is a Government site and in the public domain. Image used with permission.

Data.gov is the central site (and now open source platform) for publishing government data in order to enable citizen access, developer access, public collaboration and easy Agency publishing. After data.gov launched, other governments (including state governments and other countries) jumped on the transparency bandwagon. The United Kingdom (UK) took a different approach and launched a site that exclusively leveraged open source technology (unlike data.gov that leveraged traditional relational database technology). The UK site, http://www.data.gov.uk, hired Sir Tim Berners-Lee and other top semantic web researchers to implement their platform on semantic web technologies and linked open data. In addition to storing and querying all the data using the Resource Description Framework (RDF), the site rates the data in accordance with a 5 star rating scheme as depicted in Figure 43.

Figure 43 Linked Open Data 5 Stars Rating Scheme[67]

The 5 star data mug (available from the W3C shop[68]) displays Tim Berners-Lee's simple rating scheme for Linked Open Data. Data can be rated from 1 to 5 with the ratings meaning the following:

- 1 star – open data available on the web in any format. To be considered open data it must be available to use and modify as a third party wishes thus it must be governed by an *open license*.

- 2 stars – open data, governed by an open license, available on the web in a *machine readable, structured data format*. A structured data format is one where each field is defined as separate values with a distinct data type (string, integer, etc.). For example, a blob of text is unstructured whereas a database table, an XML document, or a Comma-Separated-Values (CSV) file is structured data.

- 3 stars – open data, governed by an open license, in a structured format that is *non-proprietary*. For example, a CSV file versus Microsoft's Excel Spreadsheet Format (note: Microsoft has since opened its formats by creating and submitting them to ISO as Office Open XML).

- 4 stars – open data, governed by an open license, in a structured, non-proprietary format **and** *uses the W3C Resource Description Framework (RDF) standard* to identify the subjects and objects in your data so that other people on the web can refer to the things in your data. You should remember that RDF uses Uniform Resource Identifiers (URIs) to reference subjects and objects. Additionally, for querying the format, you should use the SPARQL Protocol and RDF Query Language (SPARQL) query language (another W3C standard).

- 5 stars – open data, governed by an open license, in a structured, non-proprietary format that uses RDF **and** *links its data to other open data* to provide context.

---

[68] http://www.cafepress.co.uk/w3c_shop.480759174

It should be noted that Tim Berners Lee developed the five star rating especially for government data owners to understand what good linked data means. Linked open data from the government has introduced a large number of people to semantic web technologies and has moved the technology more into the mainstream. We close the history of Linked Open Data with two more signs of mainstream acceptance, specifically advances from two of the largest technology companies: Google and Facebook. Google, which indexes more than one trillion web pages, has shifted their search away from keywords and towards a knowledge graph. On May 16th 2012, Google introduced the knowledge graph to focus on "things, not strings". For example, a search of Michelangelo retrieves information from the Knowledge Graph and places it on the right side of the search results, as depicted below in Figure 44.

Figure 44 Google Knowledge Graph on Michelangelo[69]

---

[69] Screenshot used with permission:
http://www.google.com/intl/en/permissions/using-product-graphics.html

In other words, Google has shifted from brute force keyword searching to directly answering questions by leveraging a knowledge graph about people, places and things and the relationships between them. Facebook, as its competition with Google grows, released Graph Search to allow Facebook users to discover information using information in the graph. For example, users could search for "Photos I like before 1990" or "friends of friends that live in New York City and like cycling". Both Google and Facebook are leveraging the improvements in semantic modeling behind linked data to improve their users' experience.

The Definition of Linked Data

Although in his TED talk (quoted at the start of the chapter), Tim Berners-Lee talked about three rules for linked data, in a later design document[70] he augmented that by defining linked data using four simple rules as follows:

1. Use URIs as names for things.
   A Universal Resource Identifier (URI) enables you to identify a resource by either name, location, or both. There are two types of URIs: a Uniform Resource Name (URN) or a Uniform Resource Locator (URL). We are most familiar with URLs as they are what start with "http" and what you put in your browser to retrieve a web page. A URN defines a name for something but does not tell you how to retrieve it. A URL specifies the network location and the protocol for retrieving it. The protocol part of the URL is what precedes the colon. For example: http://www.w3.org/Icons/w3c_home.gif is the location of an image file at the w3c website that is retrieved by

---

[70] http://www.w3.org/DesignIssues/LinkedData.html

the web browser using the HyperText Transfer Protocol (HTTP).

2. <u>Use HTTP URIs so that people can lookup those names</u>.
   Instead of using a URN, you should use a URL so that the data referred to can be simply retrieved over the web using the HTTP protocol. We do this in our browser every day by typing a URL into the browser location bar. When you type http://www.w3.org into your browser, you are requesting the browser fetch the file index.html from the web server (which the browser speaks to with HTTP commands like get and post) at the domain name www.w3.org.

3. <u>When someone looks up a URI, provide useful information, using the standards (RDF, SPARQL)</u>.
   If a URL identifies a topic, at the end of that topic needs to be a data file in a format that provides attributes of that concept. One example of that is the New York Times publishes RDF files describing the topics in their paper available at data.nytimes.com. Another example is the Library Of Congress posting their data sets and subject headings as depicted (partially) in Figure 45.

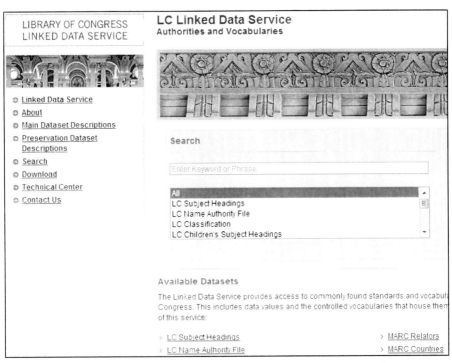

Figure 45 Library of Congress Subjects as Linked Data[71]

4. <u>Include links to other URIs so that they can discover more things</u>.

Let's look at an example of this in action as depicted in Figures 46 and 47. DbPedia has a reference to the K2 mountain range as depicted in Figure 46 (partial snippet). There are literally hundreds of attributes for the K2 mountain in the DBpedia entry. Figure 46 only contains a few of them for illustration purposes.

---

[71] The Library of Congress website, http://id.loc.gov/, is a government website that is available for public use. Screenshots of the website are permitted.

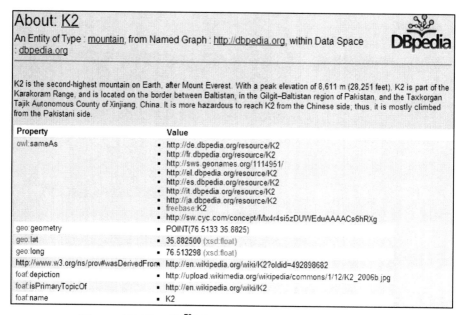

Figure 46 DBpedia[72] Linked Data on the K2 Mountain

The DBpedia data in Figure 46 states that this data is the "sameAs" a URL on sws.geonames.org depicted in Figure 47. Besides the "sameAs" references, the DBpedia entry also contains an interesting attribute called "foaf:depiction" where foaf stands for "friend of a friend" which declared the vocabulary and the term "depiction" referring to an image. The value of this attribute is a photo of the K2 mountain on Wikimedia at http://upload.wikimedia.org/wikipedia/commons/4/4b/Everest_kalapat thar_crop.jpg.

---

[72] DBpedia is in the creative commons. http://wiki.dbpedia.org/Imprint

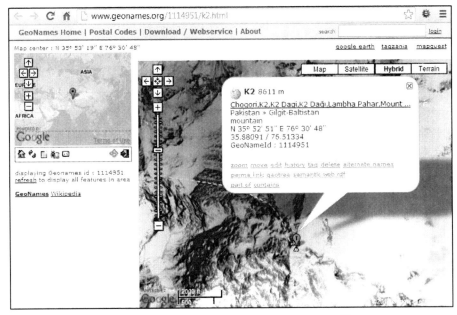

Figure 47 K2 Mountain on geonames.org[73]

So as you can see, the RDF data on the DBpedia site has a link to the geonames site with additional corroborative information on the K2 mountain. This is a powerful way to enable trust of data by having multiple sites corroborate and augment the information on a particular subject.

Now that we have examined Sir Tim Berners-Lee's four rules for Linked Data we are ready to formally define it:

---

[73] Geonames is a creative commons website. http://www.geonames.org/about.html

> Linked Data is a use case for semantically rich data stored on the web in a Resource Description Framework (RDF) format. It creates a graph of data similar to and in some ways inspired by the social networks, or social graphs, of Facebook and Google plus. An example of Linked Data is DBPedia (http://dbpedia.org) which is a linked open data version of Wikipedia (a crowd sourced encyclopedia).

Our definition of linked data provides a good understanding of what linked data is and ends with a concrete example of it. Now that we understand what linked data is, we can examine some problems with its application.

Problems with Linked Data

While the vision of linked data on the web is sound, its application is problematic for a number of reasons mostly related to the nascent state of the technology. The most immediate and obvious problem is the classic "chicken and egg" problem whereby the lack of robust, rich data sources impedes the development of cool applications that leverage such data which in turn impedes the creation of rich data sets in a self-defeating cycle. In fact, you could interpret Tim Berners-Lee's interest in leveraging the popularity of social networks precisely to break the chicken and egg cycle. Additionally, the influencing of Government organizations to release data in this rich format is another way to solve this problem. This desire to assist governments in releasing their rich data sources as linked data is evident in the W3C publishing a detailed guide to assist them called the "Linked Data Cookbook."[74]

Besides the availability of Linked Data, other problems include qualitative issues and the lack of the infamous "killer app". Let's discuss each in turn. First, Michael Bergman wrote an informative article[75] on his Adaptive Information blog that discusses some qualitative issues with linked data. Specifically, he discusses four "P" problems: predicates, proximity, provisioning and provenance. The problem of predicates refers to people using the predicate "owl:sameAs" for similar entities instead of exactly equivalent entities which can cause confusion or error. So, the misuse of predicates or the poor use of predicates is a problem. Secondly, he believes the problem of proximity is one where some in the Linked Open Data (LOD) community are rejecting reference ontologies (a formal model of a domain) due to philosophical reasons about making a commitment to one ontology over another. Bergman believes this hurts interoperability. The third problem is a lack of "Provisioning useful information". The concern here is that some datasets do not provide enough attributes to make the data useful for applications nor enable interoperability. The final problem Bergman discusses is "Provenance" which means whether the source of the data is authoritative and properly curated for quality control, completeness and consistency. Besides these qualitative issues, a more basic issue is whether there are compelling applications to drive the use of linked data into the mainstream.

So far in this chapter we have clearly demonstrated "what" linked data is but have not adequately addressed the issue of "why" it is useful or "how" you would use it in an application. The "why" and "how" of linked data are, by far, the key factors in determining its future success and whether it "crosses the chasm" from experimental to mainstream. It should be obvious

---

[74] http://www.w3.org/2011/gld/wiki/Linked_Data_Cookbook
[75] http://www.mkbergman.com/917/practical-p-p-p-problems-with-linked-data/

that the general notion of higher fidelity data is a good thing; however, it comes with an added cost in its preparation. Therefore, compelling applications are what makes that cost worth it in the eyes of average developers, managers and the public. There are current applications available on the internet and some aggregator websites that list them [76]. The key categories of current linked data applications are:

- Browsers and Editors – the ability to create linked data and view it on the web. These are the first and most obvious applications built to explore linked data.
- Publishing and Hosting – if you cannot host your data yourself to make it available on the web, there are applications that will help you publish (including transforming) your data to the right format and even host it to make it publicly accessible.
- Discovery and Query – once linked data is available, you need to be able to find it and filter it down to just the items you are interested in. The most common query language is called SPARQL (pronounced "sparkle"), which stands for SPARQL Protocol and RDF Query Language (this is called a recursive acronym because the acronym is part of the words in the acronym).

While the current crop of applications is necessary, they are not sufficient to drive exponentially increasing (or "viral") demand. Fortunately, there are a few current and emerging examples that could become a killer application for linked data. Pandora is a music recommendation engine that uses high-fidelity data about songs, musicians and genres to recommend similar music to user's favorite artists or songs. While Pandora is not a linked data application, there is a similar site called MusicBrainz that does release all its data in RDF format and could be used to create a similar recommendation engine. Recommendation

---

[76] http://linkeddata.org/tools and
http://www.w3.org/wiki/SweoIG/TaskForces/CommunityProjects/LinkingOpenData
/Applications

engines are one category of application where linked data, due to its high-fidelity, is required. Another similar category of application that is emerging and requires a rich set of data is augmented reality applications. One forthcoming device that makes use of augmented reality applications is Google Glass depicted below in Figure 48.

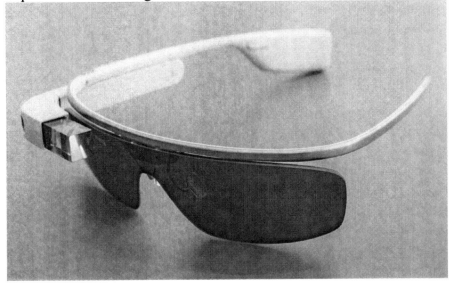

Figure 48 Google Glass[77]

Google Glass is a device that integrates a computer into a set of glasses. It enables you to take pictures, record video, get directions, communicate with others and even ask questions in natural language as an "overlay" on top of what you are seeing. Google Glass and augmented reality applications fit hand in glove as augmented reality applications provide an information overlay on top of "reality" via a camera in a smart phone (or Google Glass). The accuracy and utility of that information overlay will be directly proportional to the quality of data available about what you are looking at. Obviously, the difficult part about augmented reality is matching the real world object to

---

[77] Photo in the Creative Commons by Giuseppe Costantino.
http://www.flickr.com/photos/69730904@N03/

the knowledge (or data) representation of that object using computer vision algorithms. That is usually done with a pattern-matching algorithm like neural network algorithms. There is a lot of public interest in achieving "Terminator-style vision" where your view is augmented with real-time information about what you are seeing. Augmented reality could be the killer application that linked data needs to cross the chasm and achieve mainstream adoption.

Linked Data Case Study

Instead of a single case study for linked data, I will use two examples of organizations that are aggressively using and promoting the use of linked data: the government of the United Kingdom, with data.gov.uk, and the government of the United States Department of Health and Human Services (HHS), with health.data.gov. Both of these government organizations are demonstrating the utility of linked data by exposing large repositories of data in this format and even developing applications to leverage that data. Let's first examine data.gov.uk.

The Government of the United Kingdom established their open government data site, data.gov.uk, on 30 September 2009 to enable greater government transparency. From the outset, Sir Tim Berners-Lee and Professor Nigel Shadbolt were part of the project and established its focus on linked data as depicted in Figure 49.

Figure 49 Linked Data at data.gov.uk[78]

In working to create a transparent government, the United Kingdom has embraced the notion of open data as described in their open data whitepaper[79]. That whitepaper even includes Sir Tim Berners-Lee's Five Star Scheme to rate the data posted on data.gov.uk as reusable. Given its natural relationship to Sir Tim Berners-Lee (he was knighted by Queen Elizabeth II in April 2009[80]), the UK government has led the way in using linked data to expose government data to the public. As someone who participated in the initial launch of the United States Government's data.gov site and wrote sections of its Concept of Operations (CONOPS) document, I witnessed how the data.gov.uk site influenced United States officials in also

---

[78] Data.gov.uk is licensed under the open government license and freely available for reuse. See: http://www.nationalarchives.gov.uk/doc/open-government-licence/version/2/
[79] http://data.gov.uk/sites/default/files/Open_data_White_Paper.pdf
[80] http://en.wikipedia.org/wiki/Tim_Berners-Lee

adopting a semantic web strategy for its open data initiative. In my opinion, this type of healthy competition was a very good thing in spurring both countries to action in this important area of high fidelity, open and interoperable data. Now, let's examine a concrete example of how data.gov.uk is leveraging open data.

In order to expose and leverage its high fidelity linked data on bathing water in the UK, the UK Environment Agency created a Bathing Water Data Explorer to geographically browse the data as depicted in Figure 50.

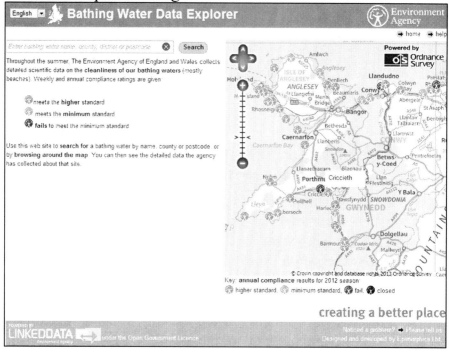

Figure 50 Bathing Water Data Explorer[81]

The Bathing Water Data Explorer lets a UK citizen discover which beaches are safe to swim in and which are not. Obviously, since we are talking about geographic locations, this data lends itself to be browsed via a map as depicted in Figure 50. The blue,

---

[81] The Bathing Data Explorer is licensed under the open government license and freely available for reuse. See: http://www.nationalarchives.gov.uk/doc/open-government-licence/version/2/

green or red dots are where environmental sampling has taken place. In Figure 51, you can see what happens when you zoom in on a particular location, which in terms of linked data sends you to another linked data set.

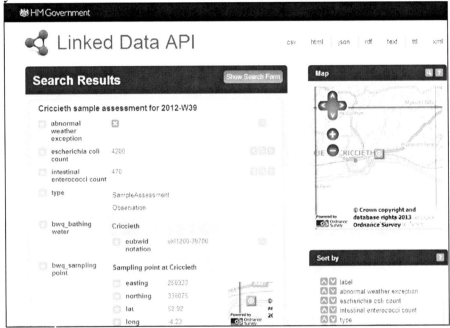

Figure 51 Drill Down on Sampling Site Data Collection[82]

In Figure 51, we see the failed water site of Criccieth and details on why it failed the sampling. Specifically, you can see the measured counts of Escherichia coli and intestinal enterococci count. Though not shown here, those medical terms could be linked (connected) to a medical linked data source that provided medical definitions and understanding of the dangers of infection. Now, let's move back across the Atlantic to examine a case study where the United States Department of Health and Human Services is using linked data.

---

[82] The Bathing Data Explorer is licensed under the open government license and freely available for reuse. See: http://www.nationalarchives.gov.uk/doc/open-government-licence/version/2/

In accordance with the US Government's Open Government Directive[83], the department of Health and Human Services has created several web sites to include HHS.gov/open and health.data.gov. On health.data.gov, HHS Centers for Medicare and Medicaid have published clinical quality data in linked data form as depicted below in Figure 52.

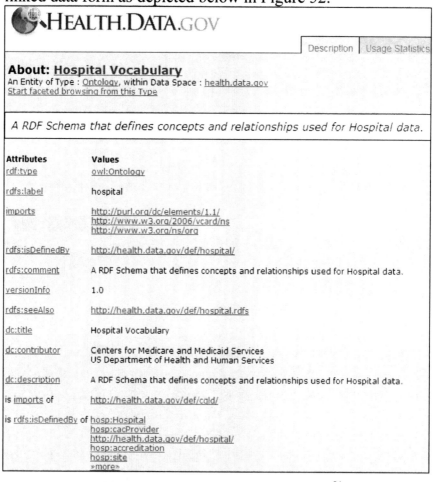

Figure 52 Knowledge Graph on Hospitals[84]

The key thing to understand about the HHS effort is that its goal is to create a Medical Knowledge Graph in the same manner that Google has created a generic Knowledge Graph. George Thomas, the HHS Enterprise architect, has posted a briefing[85] on the knowledge graph and a blog post[86]. The linked data browser created by HHS allows you to drill down into the data. In Figure 53, we have drilled down into all the available children's hospitals (only a snippet visible) in the data set.

Facets

About: Childrens
An Entity of Type : HospitalType, within Data Space : health.data.gov
Constrain facet on this type

Attributes Values

rdf:type   hosp:HospitalType

rdfs:label   Childrens

is type of   http://health.data.gov/id/hospital/393303
http://health.data.gov/id/hospital/063301
http://health.data.gov/id/hospital/053302
http://health.data.gov/id/hospital/093300
http://health.data.gov/id/hospital/393302
http://health.data.gov/id/hospital/223302
http://health.data.gov/id/hospital/043300
http://health.data.gov/id/hospital/053309
http://health.data.gov/id/hospital/013301

Figure 53 Drill Down on Children's Hospitals in the Knowledge Graph[87]

To continue the demonstration, in Figure 54 we drill down one more time to a specific children's hospital. Figure 54 only shows a snippet and this data can be followed further to other records about this hospital.

---

[85] http://health.data.gov/cqld/

[86] http://www.data.gov/health/blog/clinical-quality-linked-data-healthdatagov

[87] Health.data.gov is a government site and in the public domain. As of publication, the site's look and feel has changed but linked data is still available for download.

About: CHILDREN'S HOSPITAL OF PHILADELPHIA

An Entity of Type : Hospital, within Data Space : health.data.gov
Constrain facet on this type

Attributes	Values
rdf:type	hosp:Hospital
rdfs:label	CHILDREN'S HOSPITAL OF PHILADELPHIA
hoco:recordset	http://health.data.gov/dataset/cacp/2010-11-16/recordset/119
	http://health.data.gov/dataset/cacp/2011-02-15/recordset/123
	http://health.data.gov/dataset/cacp/2011-06-07/recordset/127
	http://health.data.gov/dataset/cacp/2011-09-16/recordset/122
	http://health.data.gov/dataset/cacp/2011-12-22/recordset/121
cacProvider	1(xsd:integer)
site	http://health.data.gov/id/hospital/393303/site/1
stateCode	http://reference.data.gov/id/state/PA
countyCode	http://reference.data.gov/id/state/PA/county/620
ownership	http://health.data.gov/id/hospital/ownership/type/8
type	http://health.data.gov/id/hospital/type/1
emergencyServices	1(xsd:integer)

Figure 54 Knowledge Graph on a Specific Children's Hospital[88]

I acknowledge that there is nothing revolutionary in this linked data case study and that is actually an important point about this technology. It is not meant to be revolutionary, just a simple, solid method for exposing and connecting structured data (like a database) on the web. Thinking back to Tim Berners-Lee's vision, the purpose here is to move the web beyond human-readable data to machine-readable data. Linked data

---

[88] Health.data.gov is a government site and in the public domain. As of publication, the site's look and feel has changed but linked data is still available for download.

achieves that and it is a cornerstone of many governments' transparency initiatives.

In a broader sense, linked data is based on semantic web technology and it is important to end this chapter by looking at the bigger picture. I co-authored a book entitled "The Semantic Web"[89] in 2003 and since then the technology has steadily grown in utility and adoption. I have seen successful systems based on this technology in the areas of data integration, business rules management and entity extraction. A popular service for entity extraction is Open Calais[90] by Thomson Reuters, which is a free service that will add entity tags to free text. Representing your data in a way that increases its fidelity, interoperability and makes relationships between the data a first-class citizen is the best way to model your data. Every organization, like HHS, Google and Facebook, should consider how to create their own domain-specific knowledge graph to both increase the transparency of their data across business units and to increase the fidelity of their modeling. Linked data fits well into a cloud data strategy as a method for integrating the disparate data you seek to migrate to the cloud. We will explore this topic further in the next chapter on migrating your applications to the cloud.

---

[89] Daconta, Michael C.; Obrst, Leo J.; and Smith Kevin T.; The Semantic Web: A guide to the future of XML, Web Services and Knowledge Management; ISBN 0-471-43257-1; June, 2003.
[90] http://www.opencalais.com/

Chapter Five: Application Migration to the Cloud

"When the CIO issues the simple directive: 'Move some applications to the cloud', architects face bewildering choices about how to do this, and their decision must consider an organization's requirements, evaluation criteria, and architecture principles."[91]
- Richard Watson, Research Director at Gartner

All major organizational change faces a familiar hurdle: handling the legacy people, processes and systems that will need to adapt to or be replaced by the change in question. Without addressing these legacy issues, change is merely superficial window dressing to be ignored at the next leadership change by simply waiting out the change agent. In my service for the federal government as an information sharing change agent, I had to deal with legacy issues and include them up front in any briefing on a new data standard or information sharing initiative. In relation to cloud computing and big data, the biggest question is: "how do I move all of my disparate and mission critical applications to the cloud?" Or, in other words, "What is my cloud migration strategy?" To answer that question, let's start at the beginning and understand just what we mean by application migration.

What is Application Migration?

In a generic sense, application migration is the moving of an application from one environment (physical or virtual) to another (also physical or virtual). The target environment could be new hardware, a new software platform (new Operating System, new

---

[91] http://www.cloudtweaks.com/2011/05/gartner-suggests-ways-to-migrate-applications-to-cloud/.

application server software, new data persistence, etc.), a new physical location, or any combination of the above. Unfortunately, most software is not developed with such portability in mind and therefore migration can be difficult and often require rewriting parts of the application.

Application migration to the cloud adds additional complexity as the cloud environment is usually very different than the on-premises environment of most existing applications. Additionally, there are no standard cloud environments and there are different types of cloud environments, so your migration options for the target system become part of your analysis. Figure 55 depicts a common cloud migration scenario.

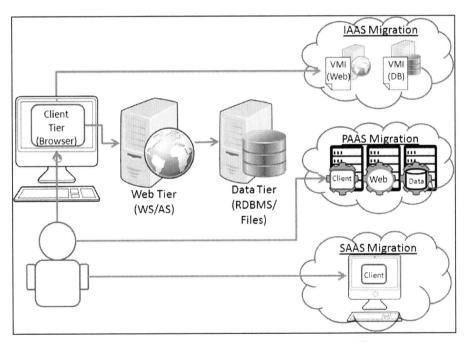

Figure 55 Common Cloud Migration Scenario[92]

On the left hand side of Figure 55, we see a traditional three-tier application consisting of a client, web and data tier. Many applications follow this model, though some may have an

---

[92] Clipart in the Image is from openclipart.org.

enterprise logic (or business logic) tier between the web and database tiers. Fortunately, the migration of that tier is the same as the migration of the Web Tier logic. Let's walk through the three use cases presented in Figure 55, migrating the application to IaaS, PaaS and then SaaS. In the IaaS migration, you see that the browser-based client user interface is directed to the Virtual Machine Images (VMI) that are now hosted in the cloud instead of being hosted in the on-premise data center. The migration requires the virtual machines in the cloud to be sized (select amount of memory, disk space and processor capacity) and then the software for the web-tier and data-tier to be installed on those virtual machines. The IaaS migration process is the same as installing the software on physical servers, the virtual machines that are created in the cloud will use the exact same operating system as those on the physical servers. This direct fork-lift style migration, will not offer any out-of-the-box scalability improvements though some IaaS vendors do offer the ability to front your application with a load-balancer and to add the ability to add new web tier images (Amazon calls their offering "elastic beanstalk"). The PaaS migration process is more developer intensive, as can be seen in Figure 55, because all three-tiers need to be re-engineered to work in the PaaS environment. Some of the existing code logic may transfer but that directly depends upon which vendor you select and whether that vendor supports the migration of your language and technology choices. For example, Microsoft Azure more easily migrates Microsoft-style .Net applications to its cloud platform. Google easily migrates Java applications, especially those that leverage its Google Web Toolkit (GWT). A benefit of transforming your application to a PaaS platform is the guarantee of scalability and elasticity on that platform. Thus, in essence, a migration to a PaaS platform transforms your application into a true cloud application. Lastly, SaaS migration is actually not a migration at all; instead, it is a replacement of all the tiers for a third-party coded application. That replacement includes the client tier, as shown in Figure 55, which means the look and feel of the application will also differ which may require some retraining of your staff. For each of these types of migrations, they share a common process for how you carry out the migration as depicted below in Figure 56.

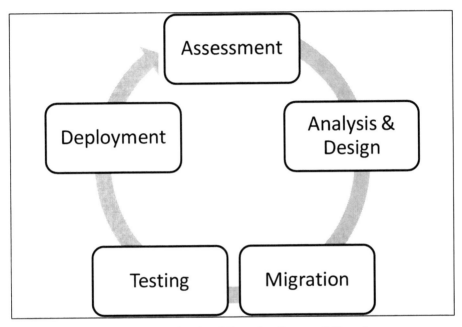

Figure 56 Application Migration Process Lifecycle

The application migration process is modeled after the traditional software development lifecycle (requirements, design, develop, test, deploy) with a few modified steps and an optional added step. In Figure 56, the requirements phase is replaced by an assessment phase because these are not new applications where business requirements are necessary. Instead, we need to assess the existing set of applications to determine if they can be migrated, a priority of migration and how they should be migrated. Here are the stages of the migration lifecycle:

- Assessment – akin to the requirements phase in the traditional software development lifecycle, the assessment phase is where you assess the complexity and readiness of your current applications for migration to a cloud environment. An assessment should follow a standard checklist of questions and scoring criteria for you to develop a prioritized list of application groups that can move to the cloud. For example, your very first criterion is to distinguish between web-based applications and non-web-based applications. Given that all cloud applications rely upon the network to deliver cloud services, cloud migrations are easiest for web based applications. While the server side of client-server applications can also be migrated to the cloud; that is against the notion that the entire application lives in the cloud, is updatable at any time and is wholly delivered via the cloud. Other aspects of your assessment include the use of web services, existing scalability mechanisms, interactions with other infrastructure elements (like a directory service), security requirements, data storage requirements and number of system interfaces. The result of your assessment should inform your cloud migration strategy to include your "low-hanging fruit" or quick-wins, your pilot candidates and your risk profile.

- Analysis & Design - At the conclusion of the assessment phase, you know which application or applications you are going to migrate. Starting with the highest scoring application, you move on to the design phase. In the design phase, there are eight components to consider in designing your migration as depicted below in Figure 57. The eight components are: application migration, data migration, SaaS Migration, IaaS Migration, PaaS Migration, Public Cloud, Private Cloud, and Hybrid Cloud. We previously discussed the three migration types. In addition to those eight components, the general pattern is to migrate a source element using an approach that achieves scalability on a target cloud environment. That pattern divides the components into three types: source components, migration approaches and cloud deployment models.

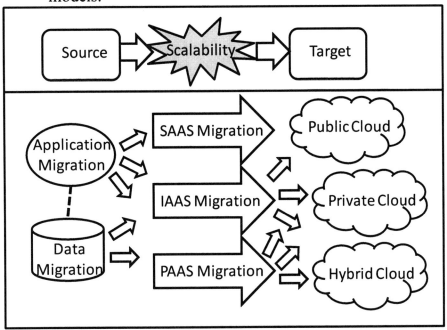

Figure 57 Design Components of Cloud Migration

While here we are only discussing application migration, an important part of your application is your data and that has its own set of migration challenges that will be discussed separately in the next section. For now, understand that you must design how to migrate both your application's processing elements for scalability and your application's data for scalability. We have already discussed the three migration approaches (SaaS, IaaS and PaaS) earlier. Moving on to the target cloud environments, again we have three choices: public cloud, private cloud and a hybrid cloud (part public and part private). The choice of the target environment will affect your migration approach and your migration design in the areas of privacy, security, cost and complexity. A public cloud is often the lowest cost option, yet may require special precautions for your data migration to achieve security and privacy protection. Another security concern associated with public clouds is the issue of "multi-tenancy" or sharing the virtualized infrastructure with other customers and thereby raising security concerns of the guaranteed isolation between customer applications and data. At its core, hosting your own private cloud solves this problem because your cloud only hosts your enterprise applications and data so there are no third-party applications to be compromised, or worse, to be malicious and attempt to circumvent the multi-tenancy protections. So, while a private cloud helps with privacy and security, it is an expensive option that is akin to a factory running its own power generation plant. Possible to do, but the lack of scale will ensure that you are limited in your ability to scale your cloud applications due to resource constraints that a public vendor like Amazon Web Services, Google or Microsoft will not have. Thus, you must weigh the vendor provided security protections against their ability to scale out as needed. Lastly, a hybrid cloud attempts to achieve the best of both worlds by segregating your applications and your migration strategy into those you trust to a public cloud and those you do not. Once the source, migration approach and deployment target are chosen for both your application and data then you are ready to begin the migration.

- <u>Migration</u> - akin to the software development stage (aka programming) in the software development lifecycle (SDLC), the migration stage is where you execute your design and migrate the application and data to the selected cloud environment. All the major cloud vendors have tutorials on migrating applications to their environment. In general, there are three basic types of migrations:
  - o **Forklift migration** – this represents simply a move, with no programmatic changes, of the software to a

new environment. The simplest case for this is to move a web application to an IaaS cloud by simply replicating the in-house servers to virtual machines running on someone else's hardware. Gartner calls this migration a "rehosting"[93].

o **Component re-engineering** – this involves a move to either IaaS or PaaS cloud environments where you need to re-engineer one or more components of your application to work in a cloud environment. An example of this is re-engineering the data storage layer of a web application to make it scalable in a PaaS cloud environment like Google's App engine. Another potential component rewrite would be to rewrite your server logic to be scalable in either a PaaS or IaaS environment. In an IaaS environment, your server-side logic would need to take advantage of load-balancing and therefore be "stateless". By stateless we mean that the logic layer does not store any data across client sessions so that a load balancer can send a request to any server that is available. In a PaaS environment, your application's server logic may have to be rewritten to conform to the PaaS vendor's model for parallel processing. For example, in Microsoft's Azure cloud platform, background tasks are performed by special virtual machines called "Worker Roles". Another area requiring a potential rewrite would be identity management. Gartner calls this migration a "refactoring".

o **Application rewrite** – for legacy applications that are not web-based and not scalable, it may be simplest to just replace the entire application using

---

[93] http://www.gartner.com/newsroom/id/1684114

a cloud development environment. Salesforce.com targets these types of cloud migrations by offering many reusable modules in its Force.com platform. Gartner calls this type of migration a "rebuild."

- <u>Testing</u> – after migration of the application to the cloud environment, a complete functional test must be performed. Again, this is akin to the testing phase in the SDLC. After all functional requirements are tested; a performance and scalability test should be performed with a load testing tool like LoadUI[94].

- <u>Deployment</u> – after the application passes functional and performance testing in the test environment, it can be deployed to the production environment. The testing environment and production environment are both identical environments in the cloud. The only configuration changes should be the changing of Internet Protocol (IP) addresses or minor configuration parameter changes relating to the new environment. After moving of the application to its production environment, it can be announced to the end-users for operational use.

- <u>Optimization</u> (optional) – this step is neither a traditional part of an SDLC nor is it a mandatory step in a cloud environment migration. Additionally, this step can occur between testing and deployment, or after deployment depending on the nature of the observed deficiencies in the migrated applications. I mention this here because some of the literature includes this step. I personally think it is better to include any necessary optimizations in the migration step. In other words, keep all development changes in the migration step. For example, say the functional tests pass but the performance tests do not show enough scalability improvements. It is best to treat this as a test failure and not as something you would

---

[94] http://www.loadui.org/

tweak in an optimization stage. So, in my opinion, adding an optimization stage merely muddies and convolutes the process. Better to keep the migration process in sync with a traditional SDLC process that has three environments – development, testing and production and clean transition points between those environments as depicted in Figure 58. Migration changes are on the development environment.

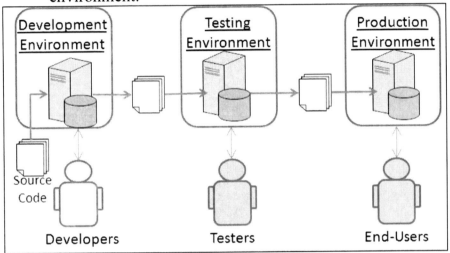

Figure 58 Traditional SDLC Environments

In Figure 58, you see how source code transitions between the three development environments and that each environment has a different target audience. The developers develop the solution on the development environment then transition the code to the testing environment when functionally complete. The testers test all the functional requirements on the testing environment and when the software passes the functional tests it can be migrated to the production environment. The production environment is "live" and is where the software is used operationally by the organization. This same pattern should be used when migrating applications to the cloud. The migrated application should be "migrated" (akin to development) on the development platform, moved to the test platform for testing and only after passing testing move into the production environment. As a measure of precaution, the migrated cloud application and legacy non-cloud based application should be run in parallel for awhile until the end-users are confident that it runs correctly. At that point, a switch over can occur.

The final question to answer in understanding application migration is the motivation and objective of migrating applications to the cloud. Simply stated, you are migrating applications to the cloud in order to take advantage of chosen cloud platform's *elasticity*. In other words, to take advantage of your cloud platform's ability to increase or decrease hardware resources based upon demand. Now to do that your application must be engineered to be scalable which enables your application architecture to gracefully handle increased workload. The three axes of scalability and elasticity are depicted below in Figure 59.

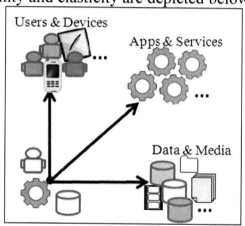

Figure 59 Three Axes of Scalability & Elasticity[95]

Figure 59 depicts the three areas where both your cloud platform and your applications to be migrated need to accommodate for both elasticity (cloud platform's responsibility) and scalability (your application's responsibility). These areas

---

[95] Images in public domain from http://www.clker.com/disclaimer.html

are users and devices which are the traditional measure of a scalable application. Secondly we have applications and services that can proliferate possibly with a self-service style cloud platform where business units can provision new applications or services to the cloud platform themselves. Finally, there is the area of data variety where both your applications and cloud platform need to handle a growing number of data types and formats. While the traditional definition of scalability and elasticity focus on increasing demand by users; the other two axes are just as important to consider. All three areas can grow and/or shrink based upon the needs of your organization.

Data Migration

Your data migration strategy depends upon several factors to include your migration type (IaaS or PaaS), the type of data (structured, unstructured or both) to be migrated, your need for data scalability and the volume of data to be migrated. Let's examine each of these factors individually.

- Migration by Cloud platform type – A migration to an IaaS cloud environment offers little in the way of data migration because when you virtualize your existing server setup that implies you are virtualizing your existing data storage mechanisms "as-is". For example, let's say your current systems run a MySql database on a Linux server. To migrate that to an IaaS cloud, you configure and launch a Linux image and then install MySql database software on it and then dump your SQL databases and import them into the MySql database on the virtual image. That is the most common way you would migrate your data to an IaaS platform. The good thing about porting your data to an IaaS platform is that it is easy to do. The bad thing about porting your data to an IaaS platform is that you have not improved the scalability of your data. So, now let's examine the option of porting your data to a

PaaS platform. The key problem with porting your data to a PaaS platform is that there are no data portability standards between PaaS platforms, which forces you to choose one proprietary API over another. Additionally, the type of PaaS platform you choose typically depends upon the platform choices of your existing organization. For example, if you have a Java web application you will pick a PaaS platform that supports the migration and development of Java cloud applications. Although this distinction is quickly diminishing as most of the popular PaaS platforms are quickly adding multi-language and multi-library support to their offerings. Given all these options, let's examine a simple scenario where you want to port a relational database for your existing Java web application to a scalable cloud PaaS platform. One easy way to do this for the Google App Engine is to ensure your code to access the data uses the Java Persistence Architecture (JPA) which is a standard Java library that enables Object to Relational Mapping (ORM). Once your web application supports JPA, Google has added support for that library to interface with their NoSQL back-end. In other words, the JPA becomes a standard interface to Google AppEngine's scalable data store.

- Migration by data type – besides your target platform choices, you need to know the types of data that you have as that will dictate your requirements for those target platforms. For example, if you have many files to store and the target platform does not offer a file or BLOB API – you cannot store those files on that platform. Figure 60 depicts the three major types of application data you need to store.

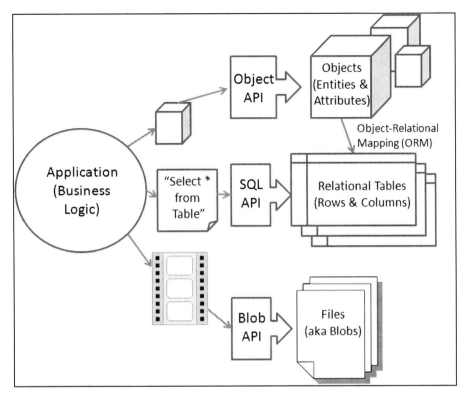

Figure 60 Cloud Storage by Data Type

Figure 60 shows three types of data to be stored by your application: raw objects, structured query language calls (i.e. database calls) or blobs of data (files, video, audio, etc.). The term "BLOB" stands for "Binary Large Object". These are discrete forms of data, the only other form that could be added would be streaming data which would need to be handled differently. Of course, streaming data can be broken into discrete chunks for storage or accumulated until a "complete blob" is ready to be stored. Storing objects (which are also called "instances of classes" in object oriented programming), is the easiest approach for programmers as they are very familiar and comfortable with passing around and manipulating objects. Storing objects lends itself very well to NoSQL databases and therefore is a good fit for moving to cloud storage. These NoSQL back-ends provide automatic scalability. Another common approach is for your application to create Structured Query Language (SQL) commands and communicate with a back-end relational database. While some of the major cloud players are now offering SQL based cloud storage (Amazon, Google, Azure), most of them do not provide automatic scalability. In other words, if you want to leverage multiple back-end relational databases to make large quantities of relational data scalable, you have to come up with your own "sharding" strategy and handle it in your application. Thus for migrating data to the cloud, this is not the best option. Finally, storing blobs of data usually involves moving away from storing it on a local file system and instead using an API from your cloud provider. These APIs are similar to the Object APIs as they often leverage a NoSQL database.

- <u>Migration by data scalability requirements</u> – the simple question here is to assess your migration choices based upon whether your data needs to be scalable. While you may think it is always ok to assume "yes" to that question, it is better to know the growth rate and nature of such growth to make a more educated cost/benefit analysis. To determine your application's growth rate, you should understand the nature of data being added to the system (i.e. form data, images, etc.), how much each user would add to the system in a typical transaction and how many users per day interact with the system. From those facts you can get an idea of the data growth rate of your system which you then compare to your current storage capacity and current application response times. Given that disk storage has been dropping in price every year, you may not need to change your data storage method because your data growth is well within your current capacity. Besides data growth rates, you should understand the nature of your application's data usage in terms of the percentage of reads versus writes. Additionally, writing data can be divided into creation versus update. Obviously, data reads do not affect your data growth rate whereas data writes do affect your growth rate. Of course, all data transactions – reads and writes - affect the efficiency of the access to your data. Thus, you measure your scalability needs based on two criteria: growth rate versus capacity and percentage of reads versus writes. If more users perform reads than writes and your performance is currently acceptable, it is unlikely that you need to change your data storage method. Given that, you could choose the easy data migration path towards an IaaS approach as described above.

- Migration by data volume – similar to the question of growth rate is an understanding of the current and projected data volume generated by your application. This question is related to a larger enterprise question of whether you have "big data" and thereby need to use a big data solution like Hadoop as discussed in Chapter 3. The simplest answer is whether your application's data volume will outstrip the storage capacity of a single machine (for example your current database server's disk space); of course, this question becomes more complex if you are using a Storage Area Network (SAN), database clustering or database replication. Although, in a general sense, use of any of those represents a more complex migration scenario that goes beyond just analyzing data volume. In fact, usually using those technologies means that your application's data volume is larger than can be served by a single machine and therefore is a candidate for a potential migration to a PaaS environment. Having said that, care should be taken for the applications that leverage database clustering and database replication to ensure that the PaaS platform can support the same levels of reliability and redundancy as your current data storage mechanism. As a rule of thumb, if your application's data storage is complex, you should first look to replicate it in the cloud via an IaaS solution and use a small pilot to evaluate other storage options.

Now you should have a good understanding of the options for migrating your data to the cloud. Your data migration strategy should be considered separately from your application migration strategy, although one may influence the other. Let's examine some specific use cases to demonstrate these migration techniques.

IaaS Migration Case Study

My company was asked by a government customer to migrate our existing Windows-based biometric applications to the Amazon Elastic Compute Cloud (EC2). In this section, I will examine the obstacles we faced and explore some of the ramifications of migrating to an Infrastructure-as-a-Service (IaaS) platform. Over the course of several hours, we successfully migrated our client-server system to the Amazon cloud. The architecture of the biometrics collection system is depicted in Figure 61. The architecture consists of three main parts - a collection platform, an aggregation portal and a matching engine. Everything except the clients can be hosted in the cloud. Our biometrics collection and exploitation system consists of multiple client systems on various platforms, a COM+ based Windows server, and a web-services based matching engine. Our goal was to migrate the matching engine to the cloud so that the clients could send matching requests to the matching engine. Spinning up virtual machines in the Amazon cloud involves setting up an account (credit card required), selecting the parameters of your desired operating system's "image" and then launching the image. Sizing and capacity planning are key exercises to get this right as the more robust virtual machine you want, the higher the price per hour.

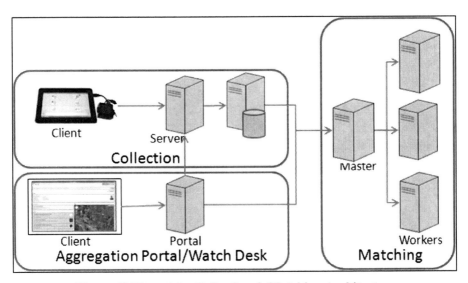

Figure 61 Biometrics Collection & Matching Architecture

Sizing the operating system (OS) image tripped up part of the team researching this as they chose the cheapest image which gave them significantly less memory and disk space than our image which made configuration harder and slower. We selected 8GB of Random Access Memory (RAM), Windows Server 2008 R2 (with SQL Server pre-installed) and plenty of disk space. After we launched the virtual machine, we set up public and private encryption keys to create a secure connection. Finally, we used the standard Windows "Remote Desktop" client to log in to the virtual machine, upload files, install and configure our software. Within a few hours, we had a biometrics system running in the cloud. That updated image, with our server software installed, can be saved as a custom image and launched at any time. Thus, we have "biometric-matching-in-a-box" ready to launch on thousands of Amazon servers in an instant! To test the system we were able to successfully have multiple clients access the matching engine that was hosted "in the cloud", send it fingerprint and iris matching jobs and receive the results.

For defense and homeland security missions, matching against massive numbers of biometrics in near real time can be the difference between apprehending a suspect and letting them slip through your defenses. It is important to understand that this biometric matching server in question was designed to use web services, so in essence, it was already "cloud ready". Furthermore, this same capability could be launched on a private cloud, just as easily as we did on the Amazon cloud as long as the private cloud supports the OS version and capacity parameters we require. A follow-on step is to explore the Amazon Web Services that enable you to launch images programmatically so we can implement some auto-scaling mechanisms that would spin up new virtual machines once a capacity threshold is surpassed. The data migration for this test, consisted of a "forklift" approach where we just ported the data storage (as-is) which consisted of use of an SQL Server database and the local filesystem. Since then, we have begun exploring the options for scalable NoSQL storage and leveraging the AWS Simple Storage Service (S3) for the image and fingerprint data.

Now, let's explore the ramifications of this type of cloud implementation. First, why choose an IaaS cloud and not a Platform as a Service (PaaS) Cloud? The answer here is that we had a scalable, web-services based matching engine that could leverage IaaS scalability without rewriting the application. Thus, I cannot stress enough that web-service investments will pay dividends for your eventual cloud migration. Another important ramification here is whether your application can afford "coarse-grained" scalability or whether your data or processing needs require the "fine-grained" scalability and access of a PaaS solution. This issue of "granularity" in cloud implementations is critical to understand in order to develop your cloud migration roadmap. By coarse-grained scalability, I mean it is acceptable to incur the "OS-overhead" and file-based paradigm of a virtual server-to-server scalability solution. Such scalability at the server (or node) level is what IaaS offers and what IaaS vendors are making even more attractive with low pricing, queuing and caching services. So, as we saw in this case study, take care in sizing your virtual machines and consider the tradeoffs between coarse and fine-grained scalability in your cloud migration strategy.

PaaS Migration Case Study

I developed a simple project management system for a client which eventually expanded into a task, project and knowledge management system which we refer to by its acronym, TPK. It is a traditional three tier web application as depicted in Figure 62.

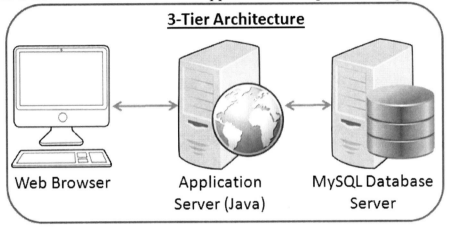

Figure 62 TPK Architecture[96]

The user interface is displayed in a web browser as depicted in Figure 63. The simple user interface is rendered in HTML and Javascript using the Google Web Toolkit (GWT). The Google Web Toolkit enables you to program in the Java programming language and then compiles your user interface Java code into cross-browser HTML and Javascript. The middle tier in Figure 62 is any Java application server able to run Java servlets. For TPK, we run the middle tier on the Oracle Glassfish application server. Finally, the database tier consists of an Oracle MySQL database running on a separate server. The middle tier sends Structured Query Language (SQL) commands to the MySQL

---

[96] Clipart in the public domain from openclipart.org.

database server over the network via the standard Java Database Connectivity (JDBC) API.

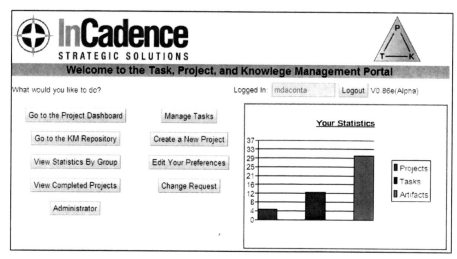

Figure 63 TPK Main UI Screen[97]

To migrate this application to an IaaS cloud is as simple as provisioning two Windows or Linux based servers, installing a Java application server on one and a MySQL server on the other, deploying the Web Archive (.war) file to the application server and creating the tables on the database server. The problem with migrating this to an IaaS cloud is that you do not get any data scalability for either the database storage or the file storage (for the document repository part of the application). If the application is to scale to many users, a better solution would be to migrate this to a PaaS environment and port the data storage parts of the application to one of the PaaS environment APIs. One downside of migrating to a PaaS solution is that the PaaS environments are not uniform (whereas IaaS environments are). Let's examine our available options on several major PaaS environments.

The two key areas for the data migration of TPK are to shift from the SQL store to a NoSQL store and shift from file

---

[97] Screenshot is used with permission from InCadence Strategic Solutions, Inc.

system storage to BLOB Storage. Let's examine both of those migration paths for the major PaaS platforms.

- Google's AppEngine [98] Migration - Google's PaaS environment is called "AppEngine" and it is a multi-language environment that supports applications written in Java, Python, Go and PHP. The Java Runtime environment provides a scalable servlet container to receive HTTP requests. For data storage, the app engine supports three options: the AppEngine Data Store (NoSQL data store), CloudSQL and Cloud Storage (the Blobstore). The Java Datastore API supports two standard Java Object-Relational-Mapping (ORM) interfaces to the storage engine - Java Data Objects (JDO) and the newer Java Persistence API (JPA). JPA is similar to JDO but a newer API that was integrated into the Enterprise Java Beans 3.0 standard. Thus, for TPK migration it would be better to use JPA to store the data. Fortunately, TPK does already transfer all data between the client user interface and the backend GWT servlets via data transfer objects. We would need to turn these objects into Entity classes by annotating how the attributes in the class map to a column in a database table. The annotations used would be @Entity, @Column and @Id (for the primary key). In addition to mapping tables to objects, all SQL statements must be translated into the Java Persistence Query Language (JPQL). While these query languages are similar, there are differences and limitations relating to their different perspectives (querying tables versus querying objects). For TPK, this translation would follow a 70/30 split where 70 percent of the translation would be straightforward and 30 percent would be difficult and require a rewrite. In terms of scalability, this migration to a NoSQL datastore using the

---

[98] https://developers.google.com/appengine/

JPA API would provide good data scalability for the structured data storage in the TPK application. In addition to structured data storage, TPK has a document repository so we would need the ability to store large files. The Google AppEngine has a Blobstore API that allows you to store and retrieve arbitrarily large binary large objects (BLOBs). Thus in relation to PaaS migration for this Google Web Toolkit (GWT) application, it boils down to migrating the data storage away from a relational database/file system solution to an ORM/Blobstore solution.

- Amazon Web Services' Beanstalk Migration – AWS enables Java developers to upload an existing .war file for hosting on their infrastructure. The application becomes available as "myapp.elasticbeanstalk.com" and includes a load balancer in front of any number of web app server containers running on EC2 instances. The code run in the web app server can connect to any of the available SQL, NoSQL or BLOB stores available from AWS. In terms of ease of migration, the Amazon beanstalk approach is nearly identical to the Google AppEngine approach and both even offer a user friendly Eclipse based toolkit as a front-end to developing for their platform. The key difference in migration is that the Google and Amazon Application Programming Interfaces (APIs) are incompatible so you must choose one or the other. Again, the majority of work for the migration will come down to the data migration tasks for the structured and unstructured (BLOB) data.

- Microsoft Azure Migration – Similar to Amazon and Google, Microsoft offers a Java web application container to host the business logic by running Tomcat on a virtual machine (though it has to be manually installed and configured). Also similar are the data service offerings that provide a Blob service, Table Service (NoSQL storage) or an SQL database. Thus, the migration of TPK to the cloud on Microsoft Azure would involve rewriting the data storage portions to change the SQL calls to NoSQL calls (or reuse the SQL service but give up scalability) and then rewrite the file-based storage to use the Blob Service.

It is important to understand two key points about migration of Java applications to a PaaS:

1. Java web app containers are interoperable – the Java Enterprise Edition (EE) server has standardized the "container" for Java enterprise applications since 1998. The current version is Java EE 7 and as part of that the Java Community Process (JCP) has standardized a web container and an Enterprise Java Beans (EJB) container. The TPK application above only uses the web container which is the most popular Java container. Since these containers have been around awhile and conform to a strict, written standard; they have been interoperable for years and the same guarantees apply to the cloud computing space. All of the web containers in the PaaS platforms discussed (Google, Amazon, Microsoft) run the exact same web applications that are packaged and deployed in a standard "WAR"[99] file which is an acronym for Web Archive and ends with a .war extension. A WAR file is just a variation on a .zip file (compressed set of files in a directory structure) with a particular manifest and directory structure suitable for web application organization and deployment of the necessary component parts.

2. PaaS data migration is proprietary – unfortunately, the data migration story is where the problems and pitfalls

---

[99] http://en.wikipedia.org/wiki/WAR_file_format_(Sun)

lie in this migration scenario. All of the platforms have their own API for NoSQL and BLOB storage. One bright spot is all the vendors offer some form of SQL storage as part of their offering which is more standardized; however, most implementations are not guaranteed to be scalable.

Now that we have seen some of the issues with PaaS migration in regards to proprietary APIs, it is time to delve into the key challenges for cloud migration to include security, interoperability and evolution.

Challenges for Cloud Migration

The challenges to cloud migration are some of the same challenges that have slowed cloud adoption. In this section, we will examine the current state of three major problem areas and then discuss some possible solutions to address them.

Cloud Security

Cloud security is a sub-domain of the general discipline of computer security. In general, computer security examines classes of computer system vulnerabilities, assesses the risks of computer systems and devises sets of security controls to mitigate the vulnerabilities. For cloud computing, the most commonly discussed vulnerabilities are:

- <u>Data loss or compromise</u> – storing your data out of your facility, and thus out of your direct, hands-on control is a concern to many organizations. This problem is worsened when organizations do not distinguish between sensitive and non-sensitive data and therefore assume everything must be protected at the same level.
- <u>A malicious tenant compromises, corrupts or infiltrates other tenants in the cloud</u> – at its heart, cloud computing is

about sharing resources and therefore in a public cloud your hosted applications may be run alongside a malicious application. Cloud computing infrastructure is often called a "multi-tenancy" architecture because it serves multiple tenants simultaneously. Given multi-tenancy is a requirement in the public cloud, security is at risk if there is not a guaranteed level of isolation between tenant images in the hypervisor.

- Malicious insider threats due to lack of physical control – since you have no control over the physical hardware in a public cloud, some customers worry about compromise from an untrusted or disgruntled employee of the cloud hosting firm. While it is just as likely for a customer to have a malicious employee in their own firm, it is normal to assume your processes are better than another company's hiring processes.

- Misuse of cloud services or erroneous billing – given that cloud customers interface with public and hybrid clouds through a web-based administration console, customers fear their account could be compromised due to multiple business units sharing an account or the account credentials being compromised via social engineering or phishing exploits. Additionally, customers fear that the cloud host's billing system may overcharge them or that a business unit may inadvertently order server images and keep them running even when not in use leading to large bills.

- Insecure or unreliable Application Programming Interfaces – besides the web graphical user interfaces, cloud providers offer programmatic interfaces to their services that can be compromised if not secured properly. There are various ways an API can be insecure like weak authentication, lack of encryption, lack of logging or anonymous access.

All of the above vulnerabilities are concerns that must be addressed before an organization will allow mission-critical applications to be migrated to a public or hybrid cloud environment. Of course, one high-level mitigation strategy is to assess and divide your applications to be migrated based on your risk tolerance with low-risk applications migrated to a public cloud and high-risk applications migrated to a private cloud (or remain on in-house standalone servers). In the long run, this solution is a variation on the status quo and not conducive to creating a single unifying computing architecture for the enterprise. To create a holistic solution, the cloud security vulnerabilities must be mitigated via a set of trusted security controls implemented by the cloud providers. A security control is a safeguard or countermeasure to avoid, counteract or minimize loss due to threats that exploit vulnerabilities. There are different ways of categorizing security controls and NIST Special Publication 800-53, Revision 4, provides an extensive catalog of security controls. NIST has recently released a Cloud Computing Security Reference Architecture that defines a core set of security components that cloud providers can add to their architecture (forming a security layer). The document also maps the 800-53 security controls to those security components. Table 2 maps some of the NIST security controls to the Cloud vulnerabilities specified above.

Table 2 Cloud Vulnerability to Security Control Mapping

Vulnerability	Security Controls (non-exhaustive)
Data loss or Compromise	Information Flow Enforcement, Security Attributes, Auditing, etc.
Malicious Tenants	Auditing, Cryptographic Module Authentication, Least Privilege, Boundary Protection, etc.
Malicious Insider Threat	Authentication, Incident Response, Auditing, etc.

Misuse of Cloud Services	Access Control Policy and Procedures, Unsuccessful login attempts, Two-factor authentication, etc.
Insecure APIs	Information Flow Enforcement, Identifier management, etc.

We will not go into the details of each of these security controls here as publication 800-53 does that and given the fact that this is not an exhaustive list of the security controls relevant to cloud computing. There are hundreds upon hundreds of security controls detailed in 800-53 and it is the responsibility of your cloud provider to implement them. The important lesson here is for your organization to follow the security process specified in the NIST publications where you first classify your IT systems in accordance with FIPS (Federal Information Processing Standards) 199 as low-impact, moderate-impact or high-impact. Once that is done, you can examine SP800-53 to determine which security controls should be implemented to secure that system.

In addition to security controls for your application migration, you should address the security of your data separately by first understanding the sensitivity of your data and then taking proper safeguards to protect it. There are two common methods for protecting your data: Attribute-Based Access Control (ABAC) and/or encrypting the data at rest. These safeguards take time and resources to implement so you want to ensure that you are only taking these additional precautions on truly sensitive data. The good news here is that your applications and data can be secured in the cloud, if you know what you need to protect and commit the resources (or ensure your cloud provider has committed the resources) to implement the proper security controls.

Now let's examine another concern for running applications in the cloud, the ability to move applications to another cloud and not suffer "vendor lock-in".

Cloud Interoperability

Another significant concern for migrating applications to the cloud is whether a customer is locking themselves in to a single vendor. The concept of application portability amongst various cloud vendors is gaining popularity and key to realizing that vision is for vendors to adopt cloud standards. In this section, we will examine the current state of cloud standards and extrapolate that to the near future. Table 3 lists the key areas of cloud standardization:

Table 3 Cloud Computing Standards by Area

Area	Standards
Data Storage	SNIA Cloud Data Management Interface (CDMI)[100]
Application	OASIS Topology and Orchestration Specification for Cloud Applications (TOSCA)[101]
Infrastructure	DMTF Open Virtualization Format (OVF)[102], OpenStack, CloudStack
Platform	OASIS Cloud Application Management for Platforms (CAMP)[103]
Area	Standards
Security	CSA Cloud Controls Matrix[104]

Of course just because there are standards listed in these various areas and others emerging not listed here, it does not mean that interoperability or portability has been achieved. That solely depends on adoption of the standard by a majority or super-majority of vendors. The current state of the adoption of cloud standards is nascent at best. The standards are all new and

---

[100] http://www.snia.org/tech_activities/standards/curr_standards/cdmi
[101] https://www.oasis-open.org/committees/tc_home.php?wg_abbrev=tosca
[102] http://dmtf.org/standards/ovf
[103] https://www.oasis-open.org/committees/tc_home.php?wg_abbrev=camp
[104] https://cloudsecurityalliance.org/

have not yet moved much beyond their creators. The most mature of the standards are in the area of Infrastructure as a Service and OVF in particular. Having said that, the leader in IaaS cloud services is Amazon and they have not yet embraced OVF or any IaaS standards. In fact, other vendors have taken Amazon's lead and copied their APIs as a de facto standard. Vendors like Eucalyptus, Cloudstack, Mezeo and Google Storage have implemented AWS APIs (the most common our EC2, Elastic Compute Cloud, and S3 or Simple Storage Service).

In the realm of instantiating a private cloud, there are four major efforts: Apache CloudStack, OpenStack, Eucalyptus and Open Nebula. All the projects are open source and their primary purpose is to enable the building of private clouds. Additionally, Eucalyptus (as mentioned above), Cloud Stack and Open Nebula are all compatible with the Amazon API. Of these efforts, the two with the most traction are OpenStack and CloudStack. CloudStack was launched in 2011 when Citrix donated the code to the Apache Software Foundation. OpenStack was co-founded by NASA and Rackspace in 2010. Given these competing efforts, it should be evident that this is another area where cloud computing is in the phase of hyper competition and both portability and interoperability take a back seat.

It is important to remember that given the large vendors in this space like Amazon, Microsoft, Google, Oracle, and Salesforce; it is unlikely that any of them will adopt a standard until the market matures and one vendor gains a solid majority. Thus, it is unlikely that you will be able to achieve application or image portability in the near future. Instead, you should focus on Technical Cloud Brokers to solve this problem, as discussed in the last section of this chapter. Before we get to that discussion, we need to address one more challenge to application migration: the dynamic and changing environment, ecosystem and technology of cloud computing.

Cloud Evolution

As we saw in the section on the history of cloud computing, it has evolved over a forty year period, with major strides since the year 1997. The technologies of virtualization, web applications, distributed computing and broadband networking had to mature enough for cloud computing to be feasible. While NIST has divided this technology into the broad categories of infrastructure, platform and software, the industry is evolving beyond those boundaries. Cloud computing is evolving in the following directions:

- <u>Amazon and Microsoft are blurring the lines between IaaS and PaaS</u> – if you take a virtual server (as compared to a lower-level operating system process or even an application server) as a unit of processing in an IT system and build a set of services like queuing, identity management, logging, email, workflow and storage around it, you have a new definition of PaaS. For lack of a better term, you have a form of distributed PaaS with the lowest unit of processing being a single virtual server. The reason you can do that is because AWS has lowered the price of that EC2 instance to a low-enough level where you can treat it like a single process. From a computing standpoint, this may seem like overkill and even wasteful because a single machine can run many hundreds and even thousands of processes; however, from a cost point of view it has become feasible. This strategy of building IT services around the virtual servers is changing the definition of PaaS as companies, like Netflix, build entire IT systems using this new IaaS-style platform. This new platform is depicted in Figure 64.

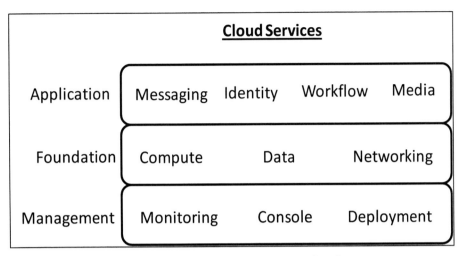

Figure 64 IaaS-Style Platform-as-a-Service

Figure 64 only lists the major categories of services provided by the IaaS cloud vendors and as you can see there is a suite of application services at the top-level. The reason for this type of evolution is that the cost per server instance keeps dropping and therefore companies are executing solutions to exploit the dynamic scalability of cloud server instances for large web applications where burst support is an important feature.

- Containers as a Service (CaaS) is emerging in the Linux community – a container is a form of operating system virtualization that is more efficient than the typical hardware virtualization depicted in Figure 65. In traditional hardware virtualization, a hypervisor (either software hypervisor or "bare metal" hypervisor) can run one or more guest operating system with each operating system acting as if it is in control of the entire machine.

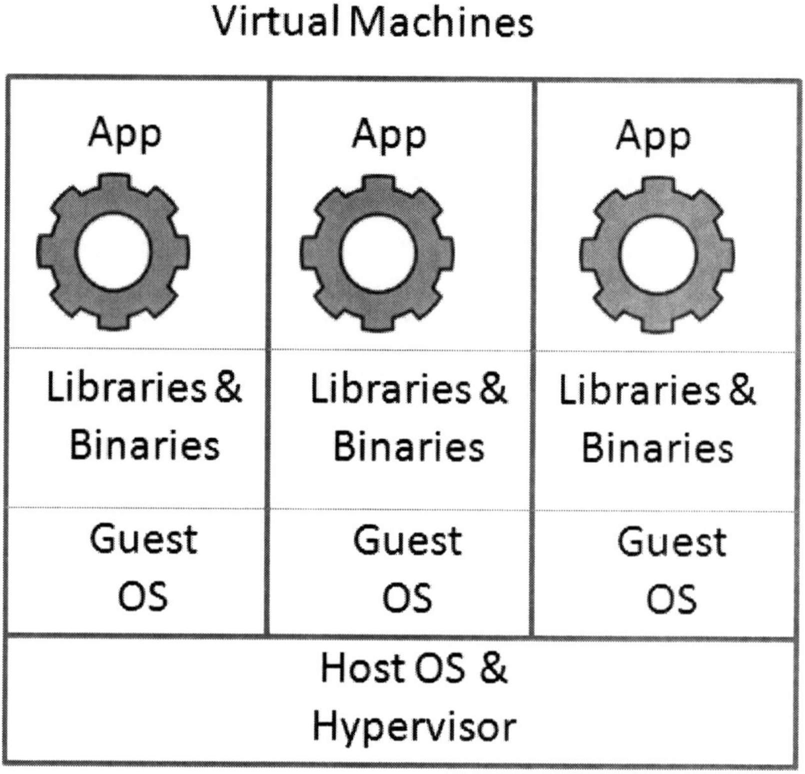

Virtual Machines

App	App	App
Libraries & Binaries	Libraries & Binaries	Libraries & Binaries
Guest OS	Guest OS	Guest OS
Host OS & Hypervisor		

Figure 65 Hardware Virtualization (Virtual Computing Machine)

With Linux containers (currently exclusive to Linux operating systems), applications can be virtualized more efficiently and run as if they control the entire OS user space. For example, a container can be rebooted, have root access, IP addresses, memory, processes, files, applications, system libraries and configuration files. An important distinction in this "operating-system level" virtualization is that by OS virtualization we don't mean the kernel, just the system libraries and binaries to allow isolation between containers. This use of the kernel across containers is similar to a hypervisor but much more efficient and does not allow different guest operating systems. A container is an isolation unit in a single OS (in this case Linux).

Virtual Application Containers

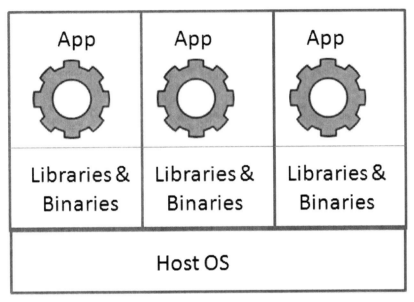

Figure 66 Efficient Application-Level Virtualization (no OS overhead)

The most obvious benefit of Linux containers is that they are much more efficient in terms of memory, drive space and CPU utilization than hardware virtualization because they save the cost of the "OS-overhead" in each virtual machine. You can run many more containers on the same hardware as you could run virtual machines. Additionally, there is no "boot time" with Linux containers so spinning up new containers is an order of magnitude faster than booting an entire operating system. So what does this mean for the future of Infrastructure as a Service? Containers are a more efficient competitor to hardware virtualization and many PaaS implementations, like Heroku, OpenShift, dotCloud and CloudFoundry use containers. Additionally, some of the private cloud IaaS implementations like OpenStack and Cloudstack offer support for containers. So, containers are a viable new type of virtualization that will continue to grow and influence the direction of cloud computing. Though they are currently only available for Linux (and other Unix systems like Solaris and BSD), it will be interesting to see if other operating systems follow suit. Additionally, as cost competition in the IaaS space heats up, containers could become a factor in competitiveness due to its greater efficiency and performance against hardware virtualization technologies.

- Instrumentation, or the "Internet of Things", will affect both big data and cloud computing – the "Internet of Things" is a catchphrase for the instrumentation of physical objects so they can interact on the internet. Examples of things that will be instrumented include refrigerators, cars, wearable devices, multimedia devices, lights, appliances, roads and everything else imaginable. The technical components of this technology are the embedding of identification technology, computer processing, and communication/network technology onto a physical object or location. Unique identification is important so that each object, within the set of billions of objects, cannot be confused with any other. One solution for this is IPV6 with each object getting its own internet address. The lowest level scenario is for a uniquely identified object (like a package in a pallet) to periodically transmit its state information (like I am a case of fresh fruit that will perish in 14 days) to another object in its vicinity through a communication technology like Radio-Frequency Identification (RFID). Other scenarios of objects automatically coordinating activities by communication with other smart objects is more futuristic and only science fiction at this point. How will this affect or require big data and cloud computing? The big data component is self-evident as billions or trillions of physical objects sending state information generates huge volumes of data that need to be processed in real time. Along those same lines, the best place to store and process this massive volume of sensor data is in the cloud. The key here is that the elasticity of the cloud is necessary to handle the bursts of activity in all these attached devices as things occur – consider a crisis situation (like an earthquake) in the internet of things universe where all of a sudden millions of devices are reporting rapid changes in state that trigger communications and thus data. For emergency responders to leverage that flood of information and direct resources to the most critical areas will require the elasticity of the cloud to ramp-up processing and provide real-time analysis of the data flooding in. While the grand vision of the internet of things will take a decade or more to materialize, it should be evident that sensors and real-time surveillance are exponentially increasing in use and utility every month. So, the long term effect of the internet of things on cloud computing and big data will be significant. At a minimum it will increase the need for both technologies. In relation to architecture, it will require a new level of agility in cloud applications due to the necessity to handle a plethora of APIs, protocols and device types into a single cohesive architecture around sensing, rules execution, situational awareness and alerting.

Rapid technological evolution has been the rule and not the exception since the very beginning of the computing revolution. Given that, the fact that cloud computing has not completed its evolution is not shocking nor should it lead to hesitation in adoption as there are mitigation strategies for dealing with technological evolution. The next section will examine an emerging technology that abstracts away the problems of interoperability and evolution by providing a layer in between your applications and the variations in cloud technology.

Cloud Brokers

A cloud broker was defined by NIST in Special Publication 500-292, the NIST Cloud Computing Reference Architecture, as "An entity that manages the use, performance and delivery of cloud services, and negotiates relationships between Cloud Providers and Cloud Consumers."[105] The use of the word "entity" makes it ambiguous as to whether a broker is a person or a software service; however, most interpreted this "actor" as a person or persons in a business. NIST divides the broker's services into three categories service intermediation, service aggregation, and service arbitrage. Service intermediation means the broker enhances a vendor's cloud service and provides that enhanced service to the cloud consumer (in essence, "wrapping" the cloud provider's service to provide enhanced functionality). Service aggregation is where the broker integrates or combines multiple services into a single new service like in the case of data integration. Service arbitrage is where a broker arbitrates between multiple vendors and the client to select the best provider. NIST cleared up the ambiguity of this definition in a later special publication, 500-299, the NIST Cloud Computing Security Reference Architecture where it clearly differentiated between a "cloud business broker" and a "cloud technical broker". In this section we are primarily concerned with the cloud technical broker, or the software layer that acts as an intermediary between your applications and one or more cloud providers as depicted in Figure 67. Note that in NIST's depiction of a cloud broker, (which is similar to Figure 67) they actually use the same diagram to talk about both the business broker and the technical broker.

---

[105] National Institute of Standards and Technology; Special Publication 500-292; NIST Cloud Computing Reference Architecture; Fang Liu, Jin Tong, Jian

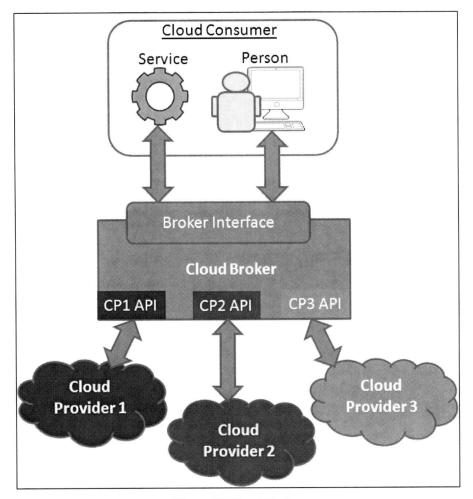

Figure 67 Cloud Broker

NIST's definition of a cloud broker focuses on three parts of the architecture – a user interface for a cloud consumer to interface directly with the broker (or some brokers even offer direct visibility to the cloud provider back-end), an application programming interface (API) for the cloud broker software that connects a customer's application to any number of integrated cloud providers; and finally the broker's interface to multiple cloud providers through each provider's proprietary API. This ability for a technical cloud broker to bridge multiple clouds and offer cross-cloud execution and migration is a very powerful feature. We will now examine this in even greater detail by examining a Cloud Broker Case Study on software called the Axon Cloud Channel.

Cloud Broker Case Study

The Axon Cloud Channel ™ is a technical cloud broker that allows customers to create any number of solution "channels" in the cloud via an intuitive, drag-and-drop visual workspace. The channel interface is depicted in Figure 68.

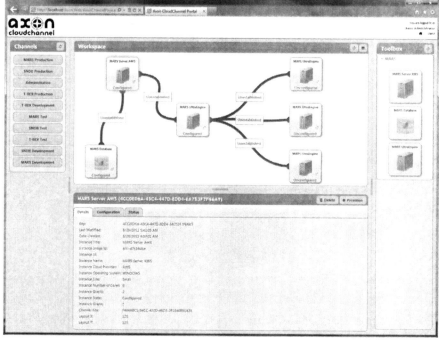

Figure 68 Axon Cloud Channel ™ Workspace and Toolbox[106]

The channel names are along the left side and a channel can represent any solution where a set of servers typically work together to perform an overarching mission. An example could

---

[106] Axon CloudChannel ™ Screenshots are used with permission.

be the enterprise apps used by a particular business division, or a set of temporary servers used in a military exercise, or a set of servers running a short-term experiment. Like television channels, a "cloud channel" is a particular view into a slice of elastic computing that is used by a particular user base. As depicted in Figure 69, a customer may have any number of channels and a channel may have any number of images from a particular cloud provider.

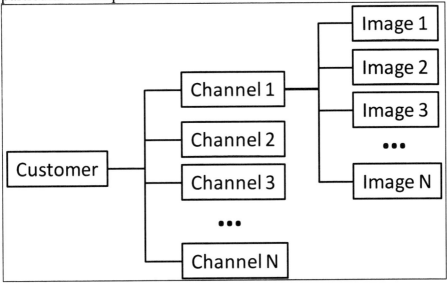

Figure 69 Axon CloudChannel ™ Data Model

Images are dragged from the toolbox on the right (as seen in Figure 68) onto the workspace palette as depicted above in the center of Figure 68. The southern portion of the screen in Figure 68 shows the details screen where image attributes (and status) are shown when a particular image is selected on the workspace. Just dragging server images onto a workspace is not enough to trigger actions in the cloud provider. Each image must be configured and then provisioned. Configuration is where the image size is selected. By "image size" we mean the amount of memory, CPU cores and hard drive space that the virtual server will reserve for your use. Image size also affects the cost of such a server per hour or per minute (based on how the cloud provider does billing).

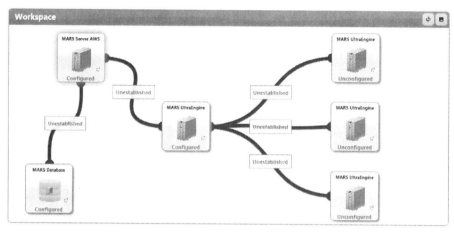

Figure 70 Axon CloudChannel ™ Workspace[107]

Once images are configured, they need to be provisioned in a cloud provider. In Axon CloudChannel, you specify your cloud provider when creating the channel. Axon abstracts the provisioning API from multiple vendors into a single cross-cloud provisioning API. In Axon CloudChannel, you select a configured image (its status is printed in the lower half of each image icon as depicted in Figure 70) and then click the provision button. Then web service commands are sent to the cloud provider to create the image in the cloud using the configuration parameters set in the configuration step. It is worth noting that the actual images were dragged from the toolbox which means they were created beforehand and saved in the cloud to be copied at a later time when put into use via the workspace.

After the images are provisioned by the Cloud provider, they are ready to run your application. In fact, they are complete virtual servers (aka machines) with a full operating system that you can log into and connect to just as if it was a physical machine sitting under your desk, in your server closet, or in your

---

[107] Axon CloudChannel ™ Screenshots are used with permission.

local data center. The next problem that must be overcome is that each server is an island unto itself; whereas, most systems consist of several cooperating servers that are linked together into a larger cohesive whole. The Axon CloudChannel software allows you to connect systems graphically via the workspace as long as the system is running both your application and an Axon configuration web service that allows Axon to pass it connection information from the other server (image) that desires a connection. Figure 71 depicts making connections in the Axon Cloud Channel by dragging and dropping links between systems and then clicking the "Establish Link" button to contact the configuration service on each system.

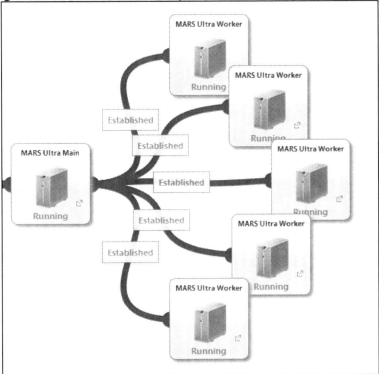

Figure 71 Establishing Server Connections in Axon CloudChannel™[108]

---

[108] Axon CloudChannel ™ Screenshots are used with permission.

As depicted in Figure 70, before the connection the link's status is "Unestablished" then after clicking the establish link button, the configuration web service is contacted and link parameters are shared between the servers. If both servers can successfully share their configuration parameters, the link is established and the link status changes to "Established" as depicted in Figure 71. This process of swapping configuration parameters through the Axon CloudChannel server is depicted in Figure 72. Both Image A and Image B are running the Axon Cloud Channel configuration web service which has web methods to set the configuration parameters (called "setParams()" in the diagram) and to get the configuration parameters (called getParams() in the diagram).

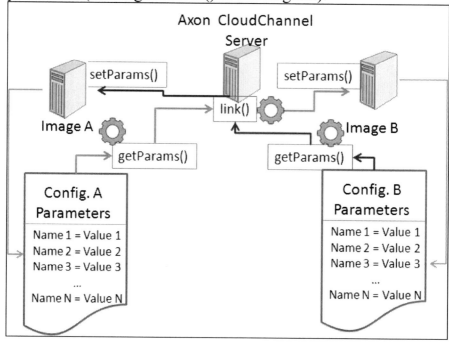

Figure 72 Axon CloudChannel ™ Application Linking Architecture

In Figure 72, we see how each Image can have its own set of configuration parameters that it can share with other systems. At this time it is not differentiating which partner systems need which parameters; every connection partner receives all the parameters and uses what it needs to make the connection. So, as you can see in the figure, Image A receives Image B's configuration parameters and vice versa. Those systems then get rid of the middle man (the Axon Cloud Channel Server) and then communicate directly. Once connected, the images in the system can then work holistically together. This is important as one of the key benefits of the Axon CloudChannel is that it focuses on solutions in the cloud and not just servers in the cloud. This kind of value added service is the reason that cloud broker technology eases cloud adoption.

The characteristics you should look for in a robust technical cloud broker are:

- Provisioning and linking – the ability to easily drag and drop pre-configured machine images onto a palette and connect those into a solution is a basic requirement of a cloud broker as was demonstrated above in our case study. I cannot stress enough that migration of applications to the cloud is almost always about the migration of systems and not individual servers. This is the primary value added feature that a cloud broker brings to the table.

- Fine-grained billing – each solution within a business unit (in the case of Axon Cloud Channel, each channel) should be able to be billed separately or at least separated out in the billing report so that the customer can internally account for who is using the cloud resources. Thus, a cloud broker must be able to enable multiple customers to be billed separately and multiple solution groups (aka channels) to also be billed separately. Metered billing is a fundamental benefit of cloud computing and a cloud broker must be able to carry this forward even in a cross-cloud or hybrid deployment model billing scenario (see the discussion on cross-cloud features below).

- Solution templates, backup and restore – once a set of servers is "laid out" on the palette, a customer would want to save that layout for future use as a template. That way new solutions of that same type could be spun up at will to handle additional user demand. This notion of a service template is also being pursued (as a standard) in the OASIS TOSCA standard discussed next. Additionally, for solution sets with a fixed start and ending, like a simulation run for a training exercise or a big data run on a fixed data set, a customer may want to save the results for future review and therefore the cloud broker needs to support the backup (including long-term archiving) and restoring of solution sets (including all associated data). Another optional feature, would be the ability for a cloud broker to enable the interoperable export of data generated in the cloud to a local server.

- Interoperability support – a cloud broker should be able to move an application or entire solution set between cloud providers. This type of cloud interoperability is envisioned by the OASIS Topology and Orchestration Specification for Cloud Applications (TOSCA)[109]. The TOSCA standard enables the definition of an XML document, in conformance with a standard XML Schema, that defines a cloud solution set as a set of interconnected nodes. In addition to the specification document, the standard defines an archive format (called a CSAR for Cloud Service Archive) to package up all the artifacts necessary for deployment of the specified service. Although this standard is in its infancy, a robust cloud broker should consider its support to enable interoperability between cloud providers and for the ability to export a solution set template to a standards-based format.
- Cross-cloud and cross-deployment model assistance – as discussed in the case study, the Axon Cloud Channel software uses a plugin architecture to enable providers for

---

multiple cloud vendors just as depicted in Figure 67. This allows a customer to choose a provider per solution set (aka channel). A further enhancement to this would be the ability to do more fine-grained provisioning and select a cloud provider per image within a channel. More importantly, once a provider is chosen, the cloud broker should enable changing the provider on the fly if a customer either decides they want to switch vendors or if one vendor offers a better price per server. A cloud that can automatically shift customer solutions to the lowest price cloud provider adds significant value to the cloud migration process. Furthermore, in regards to security, a cloud broker should be able to deploy cloud solutions across hybrid clouds where some servers are run in the public cloud and some are run in the private (in-house) cloud. The ability for the cloud broker to cross deployment models is a good solution to mitigating security concerns.

- Security and privacy controls – in the cloud security section above we discussed some of the key cloud vulnerabilities and the necessary security controls to mitigate them; however, we left it up to the cloud provider to support those security controls. A robust cloud broker can assist customers by implementing security controls that cloud providers don't offer and implement those controls across different cloud providers to ensure a consistent level of security protection. A good case study on this is NASDAQ's FinQloud[110] that offers services for the financial industry on top of Amazon Web Services' cloud offering. A key benefit offered by FinQloud is enhanced security and privacy. FinQloud offers encryption of all data, private networking and data anonymity to satisfy strict financial regulations and

---

[110] http://www.nasdaqomx.com/technology/yourbusiness/finqloud/whatisfinqloud/

provide a higher-level of comfort to customers wanting to leverage the cloud for cost-savings and elasticity.

- <u>Advanced features</u>: Some advanced features that a technical broker may offer are:
  - o <u>Data migration, quality, movement and transformation support</u> – in this chapter we discussed data migration to the cloud in detail based on several criteria (cloud platform, data type and scalability). A cloud broker should simplify the decisions and assist in the migration of data to the cloud by offering various migration wizards for the three basic paths discussed earlier (NoSQL, SQL and BLOB storage). If the application uses an SQL database, SQL migration would be straightforward; however, the other two paths are more difficult and would most likely require source code changes to the application to switch over to cloud storage. Additionally, moving existing data stores, including reference data, to the cloud is an opportunity to leverage data quality and extract, transform and load (ETL) tools to cleanse or enhance the data before loading it into the cloud.
  - o <u>Automatic scalability support</u> – a cloud broker can offer the ability to automatically scale a solution (up or down) as demand increases or decreases. This typically involves three components: load balancing, increasing or decreasing "worker" nodes (typically web servers or application servers) and data storage scalability. Load balancing enables incoming traffic to be directed at different worker nodes according to a scheduling policy. The simplest algorithm is the round-robin approach where the load balancer distributes work to each worker node in turn in a circular fashion. Increasing or decreasing work nodes is as easy as

provisioning more images of that type. This only works when there are clearly defined "worker" nodes in the solution's architecture. Lastly, data storage scalability depends on the type of storage (SQL, NoSQL and/or BLOB storage) and is either handled by the cloud provider natively (as in the case of NoSQL storage) or done by "sharding" the SQL database which is difficult in an automated fashion. Another potential option is database clustering if it is offered by the particular SQL database you are using. Again, these are advanced features and all cloud brokers may not offer them.

Technical cloud brokers are an asset to your organization's cloud migration strategy that significantly eases the burden of application and data migration in the cloud. Cloud brokers abstract away many implementation details and allow customers to focus on deploying their solutions in the cloud. In this chapter we examined how to migrate applications and data to the cloud, the key obstacles and challenges in that migration and how cloud brokers can assist in that process. In the next chapter we will walk through a detailed roadmap to all the technologies we discussed in this book and how they fit together. Finally we will develop a robust implementation strategy that you can leverage to chart your organization's path towards the cloud, big data and linked data.

Chapter Six: Your Cloud Computing Roadmap

"In essence, we are at the beginning of the age of planetary computing. Billions of people will be wirelessly interconnected, and the only way to achieve that kind of massive scale usage is by massive scale, brutally efficient cloud-based infrastructure."[111]

- Dan Farber, Editor in Chief CNET News

At this point, we are ready to synthesize all that we have covered into an implementation strategy, including an execution roadmap and finally offer some projections for the future of these technologies. Figure 73 depicts all the key technologies we discussed that must be integrated into a single, cohesive whole.

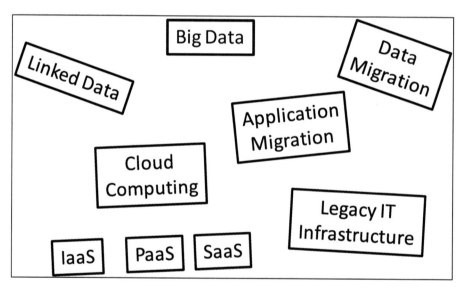

Figure 73 Putting the Pieces Together

As is shown in Figure 73, those pieces of the puzzle include the existing legacy IT infrastructure which cannot be discarded nor wished away as it is running mission critical applications today. I have seen Government organizations propose grand cloud initiatives that fail to take into account the

---

[111] http://news.cnet.com/8301-13953_3-9978153-80.html

realities and difficulties of migrating mission critical applications off of their existing architectures. The planners just assume everyone will get caught up in the next new shiny object and happily drop whatever they are doing to join up regardless of the cost or complexity. Such wishful thinking does not serve anyone well and leads to setting up of a parallel cloud environment in the hope that subordinate organizations or business units will migrate their applications into it. Usually, such Pollyanna plans hit the "reality check" wall and fall apart when faced with the first set of refusals to migrate due to cost, time and complexity. In this section, I will offer a strategy that accounts for this problem and directly addresses it right up front.

Your Implementation Strategy

Devising a strategy to implement major IT change within an organization requires significant buy-in from senior management and therefore the CIO must present a sound, measured strategy to achieve the desired benefits while mitigating risks. As demonstrated in Chapter 5, there are significant challenges to successfully migrating your applications to the cloud and therefore your strategy for doing so should not be reckless. Besides understanding the risks, there is also the question of proper sequence and order to the migration to mitigate those risks. Finally, your implementation strategy can be done in a way that provides the significant benefits that the cloud, big data and linked data offer in a manner that takes your entire IT enterprise to the next level. That is the type of implementation strategy that truly transforms, consolidates and coalesces your IT into a strategic advantage for your organization. That is the type of implementation strategy we will layout in this chapter.

Figure 74 presents a three-phased approach to your cloud, big data and linked data implementation strategy. I call this the "Triple-A" strategy as each phase starts with the letter 'A':

specifically; Assessment, Architecture and then Action. It is very important to understand the two steps necessary before you get to the Action stage. They must not be short-changed or circumvented if you wish to create a solid foundation for your cloud migration.

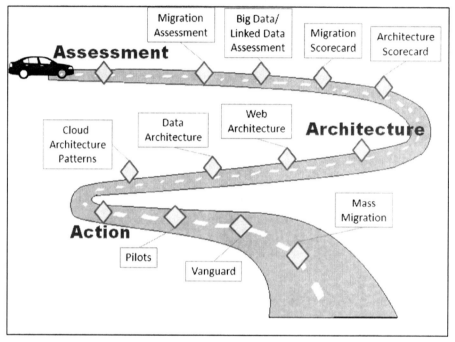

Figure 74 The Triple-A Implementation Strategy[112]

Let's examine each phase of the implementation strategy in detail:

- The Assessment phase – in this phase, you will first collect metadata to understand the current state of your applications, your data, and your architecture. Along with the metadata collection, there is a set of evaluation methods and criteria upon which to enable you to analyze those targets in the context of your objectives. In the next section, we will examine those metadata collection and

---

[112] Clipart from openclipart.org or developed by the author.

analysis activities in detail. Metadata collection will enable you to truly understand your current "as-is" IT architecture and enable you to engineer the right path to your migration to the cloud, big data and linked data. Without the proper metadata collection and analysis, you are not performing engineering, jus⁺ seat-of-the-pants flying. An example of an engineering artifact produced in this phase would be an application migration list that ranked your applications in terms of suitability for migration to the cloud.

- The Architecture phase – after assessing and analyzing the current state of your IT systems, you then can move up an abstraction level to understand and then design your objective architecture. This stage relies upon the metadata collection and analysis of the previous phase to understand where your current architecture is strong and where it is weak. Very few organizations will be starting from a clean-sheet of paper and therefore must understand how their current architecture can be either leveraged or modified to integrate (and in some cases be subsumed by) these new technologies. We divide the architecture examination again into three parts: the web architecture, the data architecture and emerging cloud architectural patterns. By tying together these three components into a cohesive, modern architecture you can design an objective, or "to-be" architecture that integrates the cloud, big data and linked data.

- The Action phase – after the assessment and architecture phases, you will have established a solid foundation to then execute an action plan of migration and implementation of your objective architecture. Of course, if you are one of the organizations that have just jumped into these new technologies without proper planning or preparation, it is unlikely you will have gained much more than short-term benefits and it is possible that you experienced a worse outcome of wasted money, time and other resources. Unlike those organizations, you will be prepared with detailed assessments, scorecards and an objective architecture which form a robust map of where you are and where you want to go. Once that path is clear, it is time to plan how your organization and your IT systems will move through that potentially difficult terrain. That is where, once again, a careful, measured approach comes to your aid. Following that as the guiding principle, again we use a three-step approach to execute the migration: a pilot step, an early adopter step and finally the mass migration. To use a different analogy, in the military these three steps would be a scouting step, a vanguard advance and finally the main force would engage.

So, to summarize, our strategy involves the three phases of Assessment, Architecture and Action in a stair-step or building block approach. Now we can move on to delve further into the details of the Assessment phase.

Strategy Phase 1: Assessment

The assessment phase involves a dual path of collecting metadata[113] on your IT systems and analyzing that data in specific ways to inform the decision process. Figure 75 depicts that dual path collection and evaluation process.

---

[113] Metadata is defined and explored in detail in the author's previous book, Information As Product: How to deliver the right information to the right person at the right time.

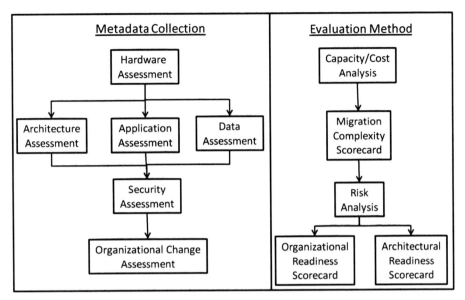

Figure 75 The Cloud Assessment and Evaluation Process

In Figure 75, the left path (collection) and the right path (evaluation) are connected in that the evaluation method uses the data collected on its level for the analysis. So, for example, the hardware assessment is used for the capacity and cost analysis. Each of the boxes in the flow chart, and their meaning, are as follows:

- Metadata Collection – the assessment process requires information on each major component of your current IT systems in order to analyze it in relation to the objective, transformed architecture. Figure 76 provides a zoomed-in view and additional detail on each type of assessment including some of the attributes that would be collected.
  - Hardware Assessment – the most basic level of any IT system is the physical hardware it is running on. Therefore, in order to determine the capacity requirements for the objective system the best place to start is to understand your current capacity investment via a detailed hardware inventory. This is especially important related to those

characteristics that are the cost components of provisioning systems in the cloud. In other words, you are trying to determine the cost of hosting your current hardware investment in a public or private cloud. The cost components of a cloud server are the computing capacity (number of cores), the required memory (in gigabytes) and the required hard-drive space (in gigabytes or terabytes). An additional, and crucial, part of the metadata collection is to perform interviews or depending on the amount of time you have for the assessment actually profile the running applications to determine if the current hardware is correctly sized for their application's requirements. Typically, the hardware is sized for the worst-case scenario and money is wasted on over-capacity. This can be corrected when migrating to the cloud and combined with a scaling strategy to handle the worst case scenario.

- o <u>Application Assessment</u> – assessing and analyzing your applications is the cornerstone of this phase. More than any other metadata collection or analysis effort, this assessment must be done carefully, methodically and completely. The goal of this assessment is to collect a set of criteria that you will use to determine and rank the complexity of each legacy application or IT system in your current inventory. This complexity measure will determine your ability, your approach and your sequence for migrating your application to the cloud, big data environment or linked data environment. Some of the characteristics you will collect are the application's operating system, graphical user interface, programming language, dependencies, data storage mechanism, and interfaces. If possible, understanding the scope and size of the application is important also like the number of lines of source code, number of software modules and number of running processes during execution. This assessment should not be done in isolation because it is so closely related to the data and architecture assessments. That is why all three of those assessments should be performed in parallel by a single assessment team.

o Data Assessment – even though data is inextricably tied to the application that creates and manipulates it, it also has its own set of standalone attributes and migration challenges as was discussed in Chapter 5's section on Data Migration. Besides its unique traits, there are tremendous opportunities for data consolidation, integration, metadata tagging and harmonization in the migration to the cloud. Thus the data assessment must take into account both the complexity of the data and its commonality to all the other enterprise data. If the enterprise has not yet created an enterprise metadata catalog or an enterprise master data store, the data migration to the cloud offers a golden opportunity to move an organization's data/information management to the next level. In terms of creating a migration scorecard, the data gets ranked with the application as in most cases it must move when the application moves.

o Architecture Assessment – just like the data assessment, the architecture assessment is closely tied to both the application and data assessment and is therefore performed at the same time. On the other hand, collecting metadata on the architecture and analyzing it is very different from the other assessments as the criteria is based upon higher-level abstractions like scalability, interoperability, flexibility and reliability. The types of characteristics collected for the assessment are conformance to standards like web services and W3C standards, loose coupling via interfaces, use of load balancing, leveraging of application servers, and level of testing including automated regression tests. The architecture metadata collection is used in both the complexity analysis and in the architecture readiness scorecard. The complexity analysis of the architecture would be a multiplier to the application and data analysis to affect the migration ranking. The readiness scorecard is used to determine the distance between your current architecture and the objective architecture most suitable for the cloud, big data and linked data.

o Security Assessment – besides understanding the complexity involved in moving applications and data to the cloud, you must also understand the security requirements of each application so that you can do a risk analysis for moving to the cloud. The security assessment involves understanding the threats, vulnerabilities and current security controls in place for your applications. For example, what kinds of identity management and authorization mechanisms are in place to authenticate users? For senior management, the risk analysis may drastically affect the migration to the cloud as the security challenges for the cloud and big data environments are still a concern of many organizations. It is important to understand that there are security controls specified for the cloud as discussed in NIST publication 800-53 that will secure your applications in the cloud if implemented by the cloud providers and cloud broker vendors. The key to the risk analysis is understanding which of your applications are the most valuable to threats, the most vulnerable to threats and that your cloud vendor has implemented the appropriate security controls commensurate with that risk.

o <u>Organizational Change Assessment</u> – the end of the assessment process as depicted in Figure 76 is the organizational change assessment. By its very nature, a migration to new technologies is a change to the status quo. Like all such changes, it will be resisted by a percentage of the organization. Therefore, honestly assessing how ready the organization is for an IT transformation is critical to understanding the best path to execute an implementation program. For example, if resistance to change is high, a prudent approach would be to extend the pilot period to include a robust education and communication program that advertizes and promotes the success and lessons learned from the pilots.

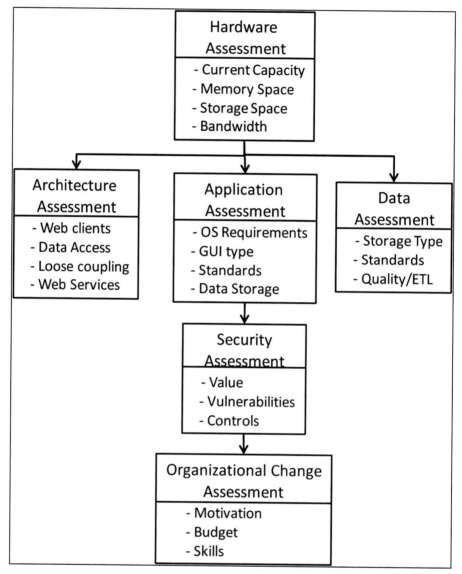

Figure 76 Cloud Assessment Tree

As mentioned before, alongside the metadata collection effort is the evaluation methods to analyze that metadata.

- <u>Evaluation Methods</u> – analyzing the collected metadata produces artifacts like rankings and scorecards from which prudent decisions can be made. These analyses should be done in sequence as some inform the others and each analysis is preceded and accompanied by the metadata collection that provides its inputs.

- o <u>Capacity/Cost Analysis</u> – after the hardware assessment, you can perform a capacity analysis of how much resources your current application and systems consume in terms of CPU, memory and disk space. Then, given the capacity analysis you can perform a cost analysis and estimate the cost and potential savings from migrating your applications. Many organizations are examining cloud computing to save money by hosting applications more efficiently.
- o <u>Migration Complexity Scorecard</u> – after understanding the costs in relation to the hardware, the applications/software must be analyzed to determine how hard it will be to migrate them to the new environments. The complexity of an application involves understanding its software requirements, architecture and data storage requirements. An additional factor in the complexity analysis is the fact that some applications are better suited to migration than others; specifically, three-tier web applications are the best suited to migration to the cloud. Therefore, that style of application would receive a low complexity score and therefore be higher in the ranking to be migrated first. The end product for the migration complexity analysis would be an individual application complexity scorecard and a migration ranking list.
- o <u>Risk Analysis</u> – distinct from the complexity of an application or system is the risk involved in migrating it to a new environment. The outcome of the risk analysis is twofold: first, ensuring that your cloud provider has the ability to provide the

appropriate security controls and secondly, altering the migration ranking to migrate the low-risk systems first.

o <u>Organizational Readiness Scorecard</u> – as stated previously, change is difficult and the organization itself needs to be assessed in terms of its ability to absorb the required change. Some important indicators on the scorecard are executive support, business sponsors, and budget.

o <u>Architectural Readiness Scorecard</u> – the final scorecard before moving to the next phase is to leverage the architectural assessment that took place during the migration scorecard analysis and repurpose the metadata to analyze the architectural readiness. The readiness of your architecture to leverage these new technologies beyond cost will determine the magnitude of your benefits after transformation.

Once the assessments and scorecards are complete, you should have a clear understanding of the level of difficulty in the migration and whether your organization and architecture are ready for that migration.

Strategy Phase 2: Architecture

While the assessment phase is akin to creating a map of the terrain in order to choose the best path, the architecture phase is equivalent to analyzing and shoring up the vehicles you will move over that terrain. Many IT organizations do not have enterprise architectures and instead have grown their IT environment organically and piecemeal. While this is understandable, it is not an architecture and therefore would probably not aid, or make easier, a move to the objective environment. For example, if the applications are built using a multitude of languages, operating systems and products because of the piecemeal approach, your hosting costs may be higher to support such diversity and your complexity level will also be higher. Figure 77 depicts such an environment where applications are built in isolation without an overarching scheme to promote standards, security, reliability and scalability.

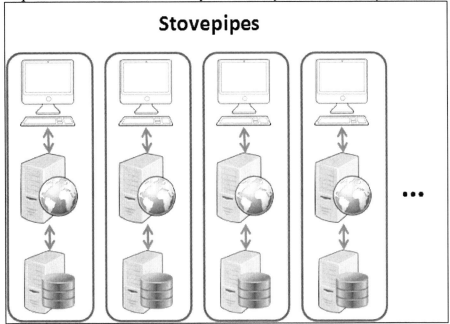

Figure 77 Typical Stovepiped Environment

A stovepiped application is an individual application that is only concerned with its own operation and therefore the flow of data is entirely contained within the confines of that application that forms the proverbial "stovepipe". A stovepiped environment is the most common and least favorable environment to promote reuse, information sharing, or flexibility. If your organization has many stovepiped applications, cloud computing is a huge opportunity to craft a robust enterprise architecture during the migration.

The objective environment is an enterprise architecture with the following characteristics:

- <u>Loosely coupled</u> – to increase flexibility, reusability and reliability, modules in the architecture should not be tightly bound to each other. Figure 78 shows an objective architecture with cleanly separated layers for the clients, web tier, business logic (as services) and the data. Tiers are separated via standardized application programming interfaces (API) and standard data formats.
- <u>Web-based clients</u> – World Wide Web (WWW) clients are browser-based applications that interact with the user using Javascript, HTML and CSS and communicate with a web server. This is the most common, cross-platform application client interface and easiest to migrate to the cloud since there are no non-standard dependencies like a specific operating system or library.
- <u>Message-oriented and asynchronous</u> – moving your architecture away from functions and towards messages, enables massive scalability, the introduction of reliable message queues, pipelined workflow and robust data integration. An enterprise service bus as diagrammed in Figure 78 is one way to implement and enforce a message oriented architecture. Message-oriented systems are extremely well suited to cloud and big data environments. Additionally, your message oriented architecture should be asynchronous which means that client requests do not hang and wait for a response, the client or other worker process (in a pipeline) goes about its business and is notified via a callback when the response is ready.
- <u>Modular and service oriented</u> – the objective architecture should be highly modular with each service performing exactly one task by receiving a message, performing its processing and returning a message back to the pipeline. The services layer in Figure 78 would contain hundreds and hundreds of loosely coupled, message oriented services. The data layer would have data services and even the client layer can have a set of client services.

Small, cooperating services everywhere that can be reassembled, repurposed and reused into new dynamic applications.

- Scalable – the objective architecture must be horizontally scalable, which means that applications scale by adding more homogeneous processing nodes. In Figure 78, that would mean that the business services and data services would be able to be packaged into a standalone node that can run on a server and new servers can be provisioned and dynamically added as needed. Sometimes that server node is a Java application server, or web server, or worker process in a PaaS environment. The key here is that if a service is built to be message-oriented, modular and independent (not dependent on another module), it can be scaled.

- Shared data and services – the key to an enterprise architecture is that you continuously perform rigorous harmonization of concepts between distinct business units to tease out all common elements and package those common elements into shared data and services. Custom services can be composed of a common service plus a unique extension. It should be noted that harmonization and consensus building is hard work that takes leadership, collaboration and ego-less compromise. For those reasons, many organizations do not have shared data and services but for those that persevere, the payoff is significant.

- Enterprise security, catalogs and master data – In addition to shared data, there are some services that should be "top-down" and enforced as part of your Software Development Lifecycle. These enterprise services provide standard security mechanisms like user authentication, discovery mechanisms via metadata and services catalogs, and master data management services. Such vertical, cross-layer functions are represented by the vertical box in Figure 78.

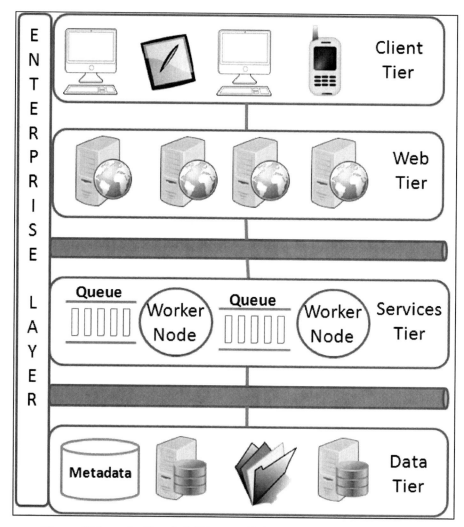

Figure 78 Loosely Coupled, Message-Oriented, Scalable Architecture

Figure 78 depicts a high-level version of our objective architecture with the clients, web servers, business logic and data cleanly separated, loosely-coupled and communicating via messages over a message pipeline. These concepts are expanded upon and reiterated in whitepapers by every major cloud vendor. Amazon Web Services (AWS) has a whitepaper entitled

"Architecting for the Cloud: Best Practices"[114]. The key architectural components revolve around the ability of the cloud to be elastic and thus web technology, application servers and message queues dominate these architectures.

Now we are ready to discuss how all the pieces fit together as you migrate your legacy architecture (in a careful, calculated way as described in the "Action" section) to the objective architecture. Figure 79 depicts a migration architecture that serves a dual-purpose: demonstrate how major pieces will move to the cloud and demonstrate how the cloud implements the objective architecture of Figure 78.

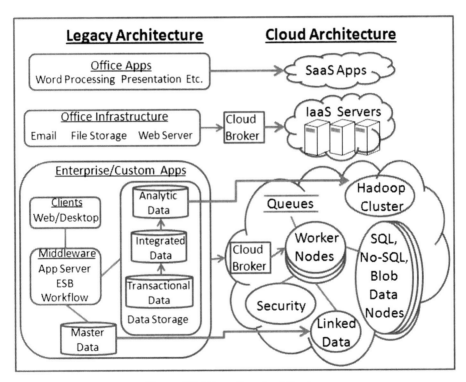

Figure 79 Migration Architecture

Figure 79 illustrates a legacy architecture on the left and a migration cloud architecture on the right. By migration

---

[114] http://media.amazonwebservices.com/AWS_Cloud_Best_Practices.pdf

architecture I mean a hybrid architecture that strikes a balance between migrating applications successfully in the easiest way possible and transforming from a stovepiped to an enterprise environment. Examining the diagram from top to bottom and left to right, we have:

- <u>Migrating Office Applications</u> – packaged office applications including specialty applications like customer relationship management and payroll are prime targets to transition to cloud Software as a Service applications. These applications are usually hosted by the vendor that creates them. Salesforce.com is the largest and best known provider of these types of applications and began with customer relationship management (CRM). Microsoft and Google offer SaaS versions of their office suites. This is probably the easiest way for organizations to "dip their toe" into the cloud computing pond.

- <u>Migrating Office Infrastructure</u> – besides productivity applications, an organization requires other communication, collaboration and general computing infrastructure like email servers, file servers and web servers. These are also good, easy candidates to migrate to an Infrastructure as a Service cloud provider. A cloud broker can assist here in migrating these types of servers and enable easy set up of load balancing, cross-cloud provisioning and automatic scalability.

- <u>Migrating Custom Applications</u> – In Figure 79, the symbols representing custom applications are representative of groups of applications that are usually much more complex than what is shown there. These applications can be migrated to either an IaaS environment or a PaaS environment. The pattern to follow is to separate the data migration from the application logic migration. In general, the data migrates to data nodes and the application logic migrates to worker nodes with asynchronous message queues in between all the component parts. A web server or web application server would be a special type of worker node. In the migration of each custom application, you examine all the component parts to include the client, middleware and data storage. Each part has its own special migration requirements. It is important to note that Figure 79 is only illustrative of the major migration options and not a detailed blueprint. Fortunately, there are many detailed tutorials and examples on the web from the many cloud providers. It should also be evident from the diagram that the data portion of the application has the most diversity based on the type of data (reference data versus transactional data) and its usage (transactions versus integration versus analytics). Given the wide variety and multiple components to migrate, a technical cloud broker should be selected as it significantly simplifies and standardizes the migration process.

- Migrating Analytic Data – analytical data is extracted from integrated data which is further extracted from the transactional data in your operational systems. This extract, transform and load cycle is well-known in the data management community and is the main method for populating a data warehouse. In the move to the cloud, this analytic data is one key target to migrate to a big data environment. In Figure 79, we see this data migrating to a Hadoop cluster as was discussed in Chapter 3. Although analytic data is a potential target for a big data environment it is very important to remember that you only need a big data environment if the volume of data you have to process is larger than is possible to store and process on a single computer in a single Redundant Array of Inexpensive Disks (RAID) hard drive. RAID drives vary in size but range from 1-60Terabytes (TB) and are constantly improving. So, if your volume does not exceed the range of a single RAID drive, you probably do not need a big data environment.

- <u>Migrating Master Data</u> – though this is not an information management book, master data, reference data and any data an organization plans to make public are key targets for leveraging linked data as described in Chapter 4. Linked data is best suited to be hosted in the public cloud especially if the goal is to share it with the public. Additionally, linked data is well suited to store an organization's metadata catalog[115] which usually stores information on the authoritative data sources or data assets of an organization. As stated previously, data migration is complex and handled separately from application migration due to both the different storage options and the enterprise information management issues that usually go beyond a single application.

- <u>Leveraging Worker and Data Nodes</u> – Figure 79, on the cloud side of the diagram, shows a set of worker nodes, connected to the data nodes and a set of queues. This is a high-level view of how the cloud is emerging as a new processing environment to run scalable, flexible systems that leverage messaging queues and other architectural patterns. We will discuss several of these patterns in the next section. For now, it is important to understand that this architecture is being leveraged and proven effective by many of the large internet sites you use every day like Facebook, Netflix and Twitter. Breaking your application into web clients, worker nodes and data nodes in a graph of cooperating nodes where the links between them are message flows is a powerful paradigm for modern computing.

---

[115] Metadata and information management are explored and explained in detail in my book, Information As Product; ISBN: 978-1432710125

We have examined characteristics of stovepiped architectures, an objective cloud platform architecture and a migration architecture. While this is not a programming book, in the next section, we will examine two key cloud architectural patterns that your system architects will leverage in migrating and developing applications in the cloud.

Cloud Architectural Patterns

A new breed of "cloud native" applications is emerging that leverages the cloud to be reliable, scalable and responsive. In this section we will examine a set of architectural design patterns that are a key part of this new paradigm. A software design pattern is a reusable solution or template to a recurring problem. Software design patterns have been popular since 1994 when the "Gang of Four" authors released the book "Design Patterns: Elements of Reusable Object-Oriented Software"[116]. In relation to the cloud, patterns are also getting popular with web sites like cloudpatterns.org and cloudcomputingpatterns.org and several books on the subject.

The first pattern we will discuss is entitled the Queue-Centric Workflow pattern[117] or the Asynchronous Messaging pattern. This is the key pattern that provides both loose coupling between tiers and worker nodes and also more easily enables horizontal scaling[118] via the addition of new worker nodes. As depicted in Figure 80, the Queue-Centric Workflow pattern uses message queues between worker nodes. A queue is a simple "First-In, First-Out" data structure that enables one process to add a message to the tail end of a list of messages and another process to remove a message from the front of the list. A

---

[116] Erich Gamma, Richard Helm, Ralph Johnson, and John Vlissides; Design Patterns: Elements of Reusable Object-Oriented Software; Addison-Wesley; © 1994.
[117] Bill Wilder; Cloud Architecture Patterns; O'Reilly Publishing; Pg 27.
[118] Horizontal scaling is adding additional capacity by increasing cloud computing resources.

queue's simplicity and reliability makes it a powerful tool to distribute work to multiple nodes, determine the capacity of your worker nodes including when they are overburdened and enable another worker node to take over and complete the work if one fails.

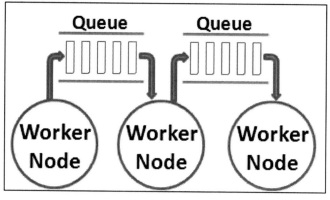

Figure 80 Queue-Centric Workflow Pattern

The diagram in Figure 80 depicts a workflow separated by two message queues. One worker node is processing a message and passing it on to the next worker node. There are many ways to implement this pattern: you could have one queue feed multiple worker nodes (one-to-many method); or you could have each worker pass the message directly on to the next worker node in the "pipeline" (pipeline method); or many web servers feed a service queue that distributes the messages to many worker nodes (many-to-many method). The choice you make on how your message flow is structured will depend upon the number of types of messages you have and an understanding of the possible bottlenecks in your application. The general idea is that whenever there is a time difference between the producers and the consumers (for example, a web tier requests a function from the service tier that will take several seconds to complete) you should put a queue in between them so that the producer is not waiting on the consumer. Additionally, you could have multiple consumers process messages off the queue. This is why these message-oriented systems are also implemented using asynchronous communication. By asynchronous we mean that the message sender (or producer) does not wait for the response from the recipient (the message consumer); instead, the recipient calls a method (called a "callback") on the sender to tell them when they have completed the operation. Our second pattern also demonstrates the use of a queue as depicted in Figure 81.

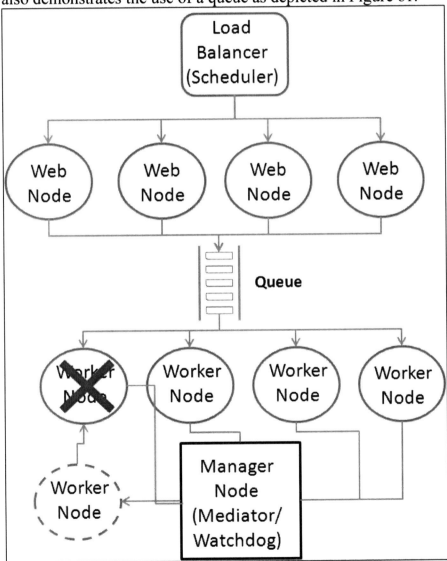

Figure 81 Failure/Recovery Pattern

Figure 81 shows several concepts from a load balancer (using a scheduler pattern) that distributes web requests to the appropriate web node (that runs a web server or application server) and then the web node makes an asynchronous request to a service that puts a request message on the queue. Each worker node pulls a request message off the queue and processes the request. Sometimes it is the manager node that farms out requests to the worker nodes (a Manager-worker or Foreman-worker pattern). Additionally the manager node plays the role of watchdog where the worker nodes report their status to the Manager. If a worker node does not report to the manager in a certain time period or if the worker node does not respond to a "ping" from the manager, the manager assumes the worker node is dead and creates a new worker node to take its place. This pattern for detecting and recovering from a failed node is a critical cloud pattern for two reasons: first, a cloud is elastic and thus creating a new worker node is easy; second, a key component of cloud computing is to be as reliable as a utility and all cloud native applications should follow this principle. A great example of this is the Netflix movie service that leverages the Amazon cloud for all of its streaming video infrastructure. The Netflix programmers have taken the art of application reliability to a new level by actually creating software that deliberately causes failures, slowdowns and problems in their production system in order to force their system to handle failure gracefully. Netflix calls this group of programs that cause trouble the "Simian Army" and have even released some of the programs (they call "monkeys") as open source[119]. The first one released, and probably the most important, is called the "Chaos Monkey" and its job is to randomly shut down (or kill) AWS virtual machines! This follows the very important cloud principle that "Failures Happen" and your application must plan for that and handle it by recovering from the failure. In other words, always

---

[119] https://github.com/Netflix/SimianArmy

build recovery into your applications by assuming your modular components will fail.

In this section, the Architecture phase of your implementation strategy, we examined the objective characteristics that a cloud platform architecture should have. The closer you can move your current architecture to align with the characteristics of a cloud architecture, the easier your migration will be. Thus, part of your execution strategy must be to consider how you can improve your enterprise architecture to become more "cloud-like". I cannot over-emphasize the fact that a solid architecture is a goal that even surpasses migrating to the cloud because without a solid enterprise architecture, cloud or no-cloud, your applications will not ever adequately support your organization. Thus improvements in your architecture towards a modular, loosely-coupled and service-oriented architecture will serve the dual purpose of improving your enterprise and reducing your migration risk to the cloud. Finally, as discussed previously, a technical cloud broker is a new addition to your cloud architecture that mitigates your risk by performing as a mediator between your systems and multiple cloud provider platforms.

Strategy Phase 3: Action

After you have completed the assessment and architecture phases, you are ready to execute your migration to the cloud. This section will propose a careful, methodical approach to executing your strategy. The basic approach is a simple one that has been used many times before under varying labels and is depicted in Figure 82. It is a go-slow approach that is called "crawl-walk-run". It should be evident from the diagram and from the label that this is an approach that starts small, grows moderately as you gain experience and then picks up speed at the end.

Figure 82 Crawl-Walk-Run Approach to Execution[120]

The Crawl-Walk-Run metaphor relates only to the rate of speed in terms of adoption. For our purposes, a more accurate metaphor would include both the rate of speed and scope of effort. Thus, an additional metaphor of our execution approach is akin to a military battle with three different size forces: the scouts, a medium-sized "vanguard" force, and the main Army. In the battle, the scouts are sent out first to find the enemy, followed by a vanguard force to secure key terrain and finally the full force of the main Army. The meaning of both metaphors is that both the rate of migration and the scope of migration accelerate as you gain more experience and more confidence. Now, let's discuss each execution phase in detail:

- The "crawl" phase or "scouts" phase – In this phase, your primary goal is to initiate a set of pilots (at least three of them) to help you resolve key "unknowns". Like scouts on the battlefield, you are searching for answers to questions about the terrain and obstacles you will face. One of your pilots should be the testing of a Technical Cloud Broker to ease the provisioning of your IT systems to the cloud. Other unknowns to resolve are security

---

[120] Images used are in the public domain. http://www.clker.com/disclaimer.html

controls, architecture improvements and confirming the key results from the assessment phase. Once your scouts return with their answers, you will be ready to send out the vanguard force of "early adopters".

- The "walk" phase or "vanguard" phase – at this phase and armed with the information gathered from your scouts, you are ready to pick up the pace. The key strategic purpose of the Vanguard element of the force is to move fast and seize key terrain and then have the skills and firepower to hold that terrain until the main force can arrive. This is the same idea behind your early adopters in this migration phase. You want to recruit projects that have both a good architectural foundation (akin to firepower) and those that are known as important to the organization (akin to key terrain). You also want a cross section of projects that address cloud computing, big data (but only if you actually have the appropriate volume of data) and linked data. The result of the vanguard of early adopters should be widespread recognition of the value and opportunity these new cloud technologies bring. Also, any major architectural improvements still needed are briefed to senior management and green-lighted before the next phase. The early adopter phase ends with an education and communications blitz to the entire organization on the successes, benefits and lessons learned from the migration to the cloud.

- The "run" phase or "main army" phase – with the confidence boost provided by the early adopters, the entire organization is now on board with the transformation. The early adopters have successfully crossed the chasm and shown the way for the main body. The entire organization is now ready for the architectural transformation to this new level of robust, scalable and agile computing.

At the end of the Action phase of your Implementation Strategy you will have successfully migrated your entire organization to the cloud. In the next section, we will hypothesize on the future of the cloud and where it will take those organizations that have made the investment to get there.

The Future of Cloud Computing

In the first chapter, I declared that the widespread adoption of cloud computing is another revolution in the history of computing that will affect every user of technology. In this section, we will examine the ramifications of that impending reality and go further to hypothesize on evolutionary and revolutionary changes that may follow. Since this cloud computing revolution is already underway, it is important to first examine where we are today in the revolution before extrapolating to future changes.

Though we have begun the cloud computing revolution, it is not yet at the pervasive or ubiquitous stage. We seem to be somewhere between the early adopter stage and the mainstream adoption phase (see the section in Chapter One on the tipping point). Given that, here is an important prediction:

> Within five years, cloud computing will be the dominant computing platform and the default platform for all new development.

How can I be so confident in this? Simply because the value proposition for cloud computing is very clear, proven and compelling. Commodity hardware on high speed networks have reached the stage where a computing utility is not only feasible but required for both the agility and new big data problem sets of the modern organization. Provisioning computing as needed with metered billing is a better business model for startups, internet businesses and soon, given that prices keep dropping, every business. Just as cheap power drove factories to abandon their own generators, cheap computing will drive companies to abandon their own data centers. It is inevitable for all the right reasons.

Once cloud computing has achieved this dominant position, it will continue to change in ways both evolutionary and revolutionary as depicted in Figure 83.

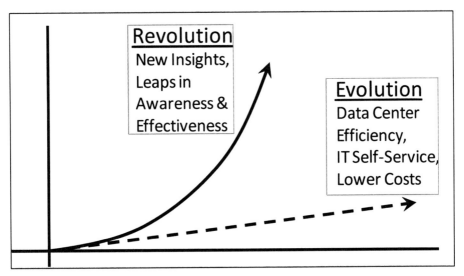

Figure 83 Extrapolating the Future of Cloud Computing

In Figure 83, the linear progression represents regular evolutionary changes while the exponential curve represents revolutionary changes. Let's begin with the evolutionary changes that often occur as small upticks or small, gradual improvements to the existing state. I can envision these gradual changes along three primary axes: usability, foundational enhancements and new technologies.

- Usability - usability improvements will occur for both end-users and developers. A key goal for cloud computing is for IT provisioning to move away from the "IT shop" and towards a self-service environment where a business unit can spin up IT infrastructure on the fly to test new concepts within hours of a decision instead of the weeks and months it takes now to procure and install new hardware. This is the natural logical progression for IT to be taken out of the hands of the "IT priesthood" and into the hands of the end-users who know the business. For developers, the usability improvements will take the form of new cloud-oriented development environments that simplify the creation of large message-oriented, scalable applications using cloud architectural patterns across multiple clouds.

- Foundations – we will see gradual improvements to key characteristics, like reliability and interoperability, to the foundations of the cloud platforms. Currently, outages of the platforms of major cloud vendors like Amazon, Google and Microsoft still occur too frequently and make the news every time due to the number of business and internet sites affected by cloud downtime. Reliability enhancements will march on to the point where these outages are so infrequent, similar to a power outage, in that they are no longer reported by the media. Another important characteristic that will see slow, methodical improvements is interoperability. Standards organizations will refine and create cross-cloud standards for all major cloud functionality. Simultaneously, customers will begin demanding easier cross-cloud migration which will spur adoption of those standards. The end-goal for this interoperability will be seamless migration of applications across clouds. Another driver for interoperability standards will be the need for the gadgets and sensors in the "Internet of Things" to be able to talk to each other. In fact many of the cloud architectural characteristics like efficiency, security and flexibility will be gradually improved. Another basic part of the foundation, at a lower level than software, is the hardware foundations of cloud computing that will continue to follow Moore's law and steadily improve. These hardware improvements will lead to continual price decreases and greater cost savings for migrating to the cloud. This in turn will spur more demand which will create greater economies of scale which will also push prices lower.

- Spinoff Technologies – some new technologies are more evolutionary than revolutionary. Like containers that were discussed in Chapter 5, some technologies are natural extensions of existing concepts or spinoffs of existing concepts. Examples of these spinoff technologies that may emerge are specialized cloud programming languages and possibly even an optimized cloud operating system. Both of these types of technologies are efforts of "re-engineering" to accommodate and improve the new dominant platform.

The evolutionary changes discussed in the above bullets will emerge in the decade after the cloud becomes the dominant platform. Now, let's stretch our extrapolation skills and consider some possible revolutionary changes that could occur as depicted in Figure 84.

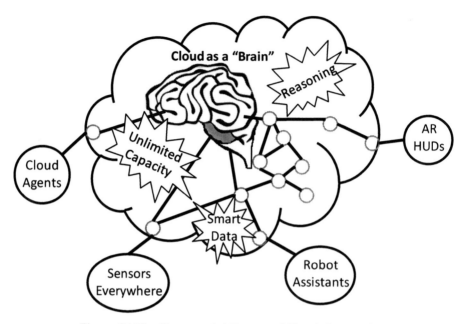

Figure 84 The Exponential Future of Cloud Computing

Figure 84 hypothesizes that the cloud will take on a more active role in connecting the Internet of Things by acting as the ever-present "Brain" that ties everything together. While I am not going so far as to suggest the "singularity" event where Artificial Intelligence becomes "aware"; instead, I am suggesting that the cloud takes on functions that "mimic" or "act like" our brain in terms of rule execution, inference, and deduction similar to Apple computer's Siri or IBM's Watson that is available to everyone, everywhere. More importantly, this type of feature could be built into a future cloud so that every application can leverage these types of functions which would be the glue that enabled the Internet of Things to work in a coordinated fashion as they are sharing these "brain-like" functions of the cloud. As an example of this, consider a future version of the law enforcement manhunt for the Boston Marathon Bombing [121] suspects. As you may know, on April 15, 2013, two radicalized U.S. Citizens (naturalized), that emigrated as refugees from

---

[121] http://en.wikipedia.org/wiki/Boston_Marathon_bombings

Russia, planted two pressure cooker bombs near the finish line of the Boston Marathon. Immediately after the explosions, the race was on to find out who was responsible. A deluge of data sources were available to help identify the terrorists including video feeds from security cameras, digital photographs from bystanders, social media sites, law enforcement databases, driving records and many other government databases. Our envisioned future cloud environment could process all that data in real time to locate the attackers in the video feeds, cross-referenced and corroborated with other data. By real-time, I predict that all that data can be scanned, cross-referenced and algorithmically searched within one hour. Even further into the future, these types of massive data scans, data integrations, hypothesis synthesis and alerting could occur within *minutes* after the crisis before the suspects have even left the area. How would such an impressive feat (by today's standards) be accomplished? The answer lies in the capabilities depicted in Figure 84 that represent a future vision of the cloud with revolutionary new capabilities. Let's examine those technologies that will connect to and leverage this future cloud and how they relate to our futuristic scenario:

- Cloud agents – a software agent [122] is an autonomous computer program that acts on behalf of a person or organization. While software agents exist today, like Apple's "Siri" personal assistant for the iPhone®, they are still of limited capability. In the distant cloud future, cloud agents will leverage the revolutionary capabilities represented by the sun bursts in Figure 84 to include unlimited capacity, smart data and reasoning. Unlimited capacity means that an agent, through auto-scaling, could increase its compute capacity, storage capacity and network capacity on an as-needed basis depending on the task assigned to it by its human master. So, searching all

---

[122] http://en.wikipedia.org/wiki/Software_agent

the video feeds at the Boston Marathon finish line within a five minute period is possible by massively auto-scaling the number of compute nodes used and amount of memory per compute node. This task would have been communicated to the assistant via natural language. The personal assistant client on the smart phone talks to the cloud on the back-end which has the ability to reason and search massive data stores of knowledge. Those data stores would be encoded using a technique called "Smart Data". Smart Data is data that is "application-independent, composable, classified, and part of a larger information ecosystem (ontology)."[123] Smart data is semantically rich data with relationship information, class hierarchies and attributes, of which linked data is one form, that can be leveraged in reasoning algorithms to deduce new information, logical anomalies and inconsistencies (for example, a person cannot be in the set of men and women at the same time). Finally, these cloud agents will use automated reasoning techniques like deduction, induction, business rules execution and inference to mimic the capabilities of the human brain. In the distant cloud future, these functions – which equate to an advanced version of IBM's Watson and Apple's Siri, will be open sourced and freely available as a standard cloud service. The open cloud platform of the future will be amazingly advanced and able to understand routine concepts like geography, events like a dinner date, and inferences like "my 'brother' is also my son's 'uncle'".

- <u>Sensors everywhere</u> – in the distant cloud future, sensors will have moved beyond our mobile phones and into every aspect of our lives into what is called the "Internet of Things". Sensors will be in our automobiles, appliances, roads, buildings, bridges, products, scales,

---

[123] Daconta et. al; <u>The Semantic Web: A Guide to the Future of XML, Web Services and Knowledge Management</u>; John Wiley & Sons, Inc.; Pg 4.

mass-transit, shipping and many others. These sensors on our infrastructure, on ourselves and our environments will all report in real-time to the cloud and be understood in their context, connected and corroborated with other sensors, and networked into chains for higher-level behaviors. The "glue" tying these sensors together is the cloud and that future cloud will drive the explosion of collaborating sensors by giving them the means, the smart data and the reasoning to multiply their capabilities. Agents will use these sensor networks to fulfill tasks by getting real-time data or to test hypotheses. So, the cloud will spur the capabilities of sensor networks and sensor networks will spur new capabilities of the cloud in a self-reinforcing upward spiral.

- <u>Robot assistants</u> – combining both intelligent agents and sensors into packages that manipulate our physical world brings us to the rise of robots. Because they interact with the physical world, robotic assistants like driverless cars, drones, humanoid servant robots and numerous types of worker bots will all require a very high-level of precision to ensure reliability, safety and competence. Precision requires collaboration with sensors, smart data for context and reasoning. Even more impressive than precision will be the ability for robots to learn and respond to novel situations by tapping into the unlimited capacity of the future cloud. Machine learning in the cloud could enable these robotic assistants to move beyond routine instructions when necessary.

- <u>Augmented Reality (AR) Heads-up Displays (HuDs)</u> – in our cloud future, our glasses, contact lenses and maybe even our retinas will be instrumented with an augmented reality layer to improve our situational awareness. Augmented reality[124] is a set of computer generated data

---

[124] http://en.wikipedia.org/wiki/Augmented_reality

that overlays a view of the physical world in order to *augment* or enhance that reality. The days of forgetting a face at a business meeting, getting lost in a strange city or not understanding the choices on a dinner menu will be over. Like the cockpit of a fighter jet, you will have complete knowledge of your surrounding environment in real time. And what will you do with this enhanced situational awareness? Connect and communicate with sensors, task your cloud agents and task your robotic assistants!

The future of cloud computing is very bright. In this section we have examined both evolutionary and revolutionary changes to cloud computing that will radically affect the IT landscape. Your journey into that future begins with a solid implementation roadmap! At this point, you are ready to face that future.

Conclusion

"Cloud is about how you do computing,
not where you do computing."
- Paul Maritz, CEO of VMware

In this chapter, we will review the key highlights of each chapter and note your "takeaways" or lessons to be learned from the content.

- Chapter One: Yet Another Computing Revolution – this short chapter details why cloud computing is another revolution in computing, what that means and when the "tipping point" will occur.
  The key takeaway should be that every member of your IT staff should be educated on this new revolution and your Chief Information Officer (CIO) should brief senior management on the impacts and benefits of these new technologies on your organization.

- Chapter Two: Cloud 101 – this chapter uses a solid, building block approach to answer the question "What is Cloud Computing?" The method used is to begin with the derivation of the term and walk through its history in detail. Secondly, we examined popular definitions of the term (especially NIST's definition) and examples of its implementation. NIST's definition of cloud computing uses a 3-4-5 model with three service models (SaaS, IaaS and PaaS), four deployment models (public, private, community and hybrid), and five characteristics (on-demand self-service, broad network access, resource pooling, rapid elasticity, and measured service). Finally, we constructed our own definition. That definition is:
  "Cloud computing is the centralization of computing services, delivered over a network, that offers greater

hardware efficiency, improved data sharing across applications, and application scalability. Cloud computing is implemented via multiple techniques to include virtualization, parallel processing across many commodity computers and new forms of data storage. A good analogy for this shift is when businesses moved from on-site power generation to electric utilities for reliable, inexpensive power."

The key takeaways from this chapter are to first understand how the cloud was a natural progression of techniques over a forty-year span; second, to understand (at a deep level) NIST's definition of cloud computing; and third to be able to explain cloud computing to others in your organizations. If you can teach others what cloud computing is then you truly understand it. My goal would be for you to be able to do a solid, hour-long "brown-bag" training session on cloud computing for your co-workers. Additionally, since many organizations begin their cloud journey with Infrastructure as a Service (IaaS), you need to have a solid grasp of virtualization as it is the centerpiece of computing as a utility. And lastly, that computing as a utility, with elasticity and metered service, has never been done before and will literally change computing forever.

- Chapter Three: Big Data 101 – this chapter follows and expands the building block approach introduced in the previous chapter. The base process is to explore the concept, then its history, then popular definitions and culminate the exploration by crafting a custom definition.
  We introduced the concept with a diagram that portrayed the motivation for big data with a cycle where huge data volumes are processed by the "data cloud" to produce "data-driven decisions". This cycle is important because without a clear eye on the desired outcome, it is easy to

get caught up just doing "stuff" without producing results. The history of big data traced its roots in data warehouses and especially highlighted the role of Google in introducing the Google File System and the MapReduce Parallel Processing Framework. The definition of Big Data begins with the explanation of Volume, Velocity and Variety and ends with the development of this custom definition:

"Big Data is the application of new techniques and platforms to process, analyze and visualize huge volumes of data that are beyond the ability of traditional methods to process in near real time. Some of these techniques leverage cloud computing and create what is called the "data cloud". The purpose of big data is to extract trends, patterns and insights from the data in order to improve organizational decision making. An example of Big Data is the processing of click stream data on a website, using a Hadoop cluster, to understand customers buying patterns."

After defining Big Data, this chapter delved deeper into the subject by examining how it is implemented (especially the Hadoop ecosystem), other data storage mechanisms (like key-value stores), the critical role of the data scientist in the process, and ended with a detailed case study.

The key takeaway lessons are:
- Data volume growth is exponential.
- The implementation platform of choice is by far the Hadoop platform. Simply stated, "Big Data" means you use Hadoop.
- A data scientist or group of data scientists is a non-negotiable prerequisite to a Big Data project.
- Big Data, as demonstrated by the 2012 Obama campaign, is making huge impacts to businesses, organizations and Government agencies.

- <u>Chapter Four: Linked Data 101</u> – this chapter follows the same successful formula as the previous two for building up your understanding of this new technology. It answers the question, "What is Linked Data?" First, it explores the derivation of the term and concept (especially Linked Open Data, S-P-O statements and Social Graphs); second, we took a tour of the history of linked data to understand its influences like the Semantic Web, Facebook, data.gov and the Google Knowledge Graph; third, we crafted the following custom definition:

  "Linked Data is a use case for semantically rich data stored on the web in a Resource Description Framework (RDF) format. It creates a graph of data similar to and in some ways inspired by the social networks, or social graphs, of Facebook and Google Plus. An example of Linked Data is DBPedia (http://dbpedia.org) which is a linked open data version of Wikipedia (a crowd sourced encyclopedia)."

  After defining linked data, the chapter continues the explanation of the topic by adding a set of problems with the technology and a detailed case study (on data.gov.uk and health.data.gov).

  The key takeaways for this chapter are as follows:
  - Linked data is well suited for publicly releasable data and your organization's master data.
  - Both the cloud and big data will leverage the knowledge available via linked data.
  - The semantic web vision espoused by Sir Tim Berners-Lee is finally being realized.

- <u>Chapter Five: Application Migration to the Cloud</u> – this chapter, and the next one, move beyond 101-level concepts towards applying that knowledge to the task of migrating your legacy architecture to this new environment. That new environment is composed of a cloud platform with support for Big Data and Linked Data. This chapter is the cornerstone of the book and should be read carefully. The chapter begins by answering the question "What is Application Migration?" by examining three common migration scenarios. The chapter introduces and walks the reader through the application migration process that consists of the following steps – Assessment, Analysis & Design, Migration, Testing and Deployment. The Migration execution section explains Forklift migration, component re-engineering, and Application Rewrite. After working through the details of application migration, it shifts to data migration. Data migration is broken down by cloud platform type, data types, scalability requirements and data volume. To demonstrate application migration, we examine two case studies: one on IaaS migration and the other on PaaS migration. After the case studies, we examine the challenges and obstacles to cloud migration including cloud security, cloud interoperability and cloud evolution. Finally, the chapter concludes with a detailed discussion and case study on cloud brokers, especially Cloud Technical Brokers.

The key takeaways from this chapter are:

- o To achieve the benefits of cloud computing on a large scale you must migrate your applications to the cloud.
- o Migrating your applications to the cloud affords your organization elasticity and agility. Migrating your data to the cloud affords your organization Enterprise Information Management (EIM) and integration.
- o Fork-lift style migration is a good starting point for most organizations to achieve greater data center efficiency; however, you will not get any scalability or elasticity benefits.

- The application migration process is modeled after the traditional software development lifecycle (SDLC).
- There are many options in application migration like what to migrate (components, data, application, both); how to migrate (fork-lift, re-engineer, rewrite); and where to migrate to (private, public or hybrid cloud).
- The migration process also uses three distinct environments: Development, Testing and Production.
- If your data volume will not surpass the capacity of a single server (with RAID drive), you do *not* have Big Data.
- When performing an IaaS migration, take care in sizing your virtual machines.
- PaaS data migration uses proprietary APIs.
- You must perform a security risk assessment before migrating your applications to the cloud.
- Currently, cloud standards adoption is nascent at best. Thus, organizations should look to cloud brokers for application portability.
- Containers as a Service is a significant challenger to traditional virtualization for Linux-based applications.
- A technical cloud broker bridges multiple clouds and offers cross-cloud execution and migration.
- Technical cloud brokers are an important asset to your organization's cloud migration strategy that significantly eases the burden of application and data migration in the cloud.

- <u>Chapter Six: Your Cloud Computing Roadmap</u> – in this chapter, we put all the pieces together and assembled a robust implementation strategy. The chapter begins by presenting a three-phased approach which I call the "Triple-A" strategy: Assessment, Architecture and then Action. We then describe and delve into the details of each phase. The assessment phase involves the collection of metadata about your current state (hardware, applications, data, etc.) and then uses that data in different types of analysis and scoring methods. After the assessment phase is explained in detail, we move on to the Architecture phase. The architecture phase is where you assess your current architecture, understand the objective cloud platform architecture and then create a strategy to align the two. The architecture section begins with a comparison of the typical stovepiped architecture to the characteristics of the objective cloud platform architecture. After examining those objective characteristics, the chapter covers how legacy components migrate to a cloud platform architecture and then how new "cloud native" applications leverage cloud architectural patterns. Finally, in the Action phase I describe a Crawl-Walk-Run approach to executing your cloud migration strategy. The chapter concludes with a discussion of the future of cloud computing by examining some of the possible evolutionary and revolutionary changes in our IT future. The key takeaways from this chapter are:

- o The Triple-A strategy of Assessment, Architecture and then Action is a sound, measured strategy for migrating to the cloud.
- o The application assessment is the linchpin to the entire assessment phase and allows you to create a complexity ranking of all your applications.
- o The data assessment task is also an opportunity for data quality, integration, metadata tagging and harmonization in its move to the cloud. This opportunity should not be lost due to haste.

- o For senior management, the risk analysis may affect the migration of applications to the cloud.
- o The modern cloud platform architecture is a new way of architecting applications and systems that leverage many integration and middleware best practices.
- o Analytical data is a key potential target for migration to a big data environment.
- o Master data and publicly releasable data are targets to migrate to a linked data environment.
- o Cloud architectural patterns should be leveraged to build "cloud native" applications.
- o The Crawl-Walk-Run approach is a proven and prudent execution strategy.
- o The purpose of pilots is to answer and resolve your "unknowns".
- o In the "walk" phase you want to recruit projects that have both a good architectural foundation and are known as important to the organization.
- o Within five years, cloud computing will be the dominant computing platform and the default platform for all new development.

Now you are ready to leverage your newfound understanding of cloud computing, big data and linked data to forge your organization's migration strategy to the cloud. You should also have the confidence to then execute that strategy using a Crawl-Walk-Run approach to drastically improve your organization's IT infrastructure. You will be able to lead your organization into this new era of "Computing as a Utility" and reap the significant, strategic benefits the Cloud offers. It is time for you to begin that journey… and succeed.

Index

N

O

P

U

V

T

W

X

Y

Z

CPSIA information can be obtained at www.ICGtesting.com
Printed in the USA
LVOW07s0834250914

405832LV00002B/410/P

9 781478 722557